PRESENTED TO:

_____

FROM:

_____

DATE:

_____

Published in Nashville, Tennessee by Thomas Nelson.
Thomas Nelson is a registered trademark of Thomas Nelson, Inc.

Thomas Nelson, Inc., titles may be purchased in bulk for educational,
business, fundraising, or sales promotional use. For information,
please e-mail SpecialMarkets@ThomasNelson.com

Cover Design by Chris Ward
Typeset by Thinkpen Design, Inc., www.thinkpendesign.com

ISBN: 978-1-4041-8695-8

Printed in China

11 12 13 14 15 [RRD] 9 8 7 6 5

I dedicate this book to Jesus,
my living Savior-God!

Having loved His own who were in the world,
He loved them to the end.

JOHN 13:1 NKJV

"He is not here, for He has risen,
just as He said . . ."

MATTHEW 28:6 NASB

Special thanks go to Kris Bearss—my project director, editor, and much more. She wore many hats and made significant contributions to this project. I also want to thank Laura Minchew and Lisa Stilwell for their guidance, patience, and encouragement. I feel privileged to work with such a great team.

Jesus Lives

Sarah Young

THOMAS NELSON
Since 1798

NASHVILLE   DALLAS   MEXICO CITY   RIO DE JANEIRO

A Guide to Themes in *Jesus Lives*

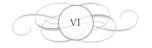

Introduction

Neither death nor life, neither angels nor demons, neither the present nor the future, nor any powers, neither height nor depth, nor anything else in all creation, will be able to separate us from the love of God that is in Christ Jesus our Lord (Romans 8:38–39). Let these powerful verses inflame your heart and explode like fireworks in your mind. Nothing in all creation can separate us from Jesus' Love!

We inhabit a world where separations abound: parents from children, husbands from wives, friends from friends, childhood dreams from adult realities, and so on. But there is a devastating disconnection that Christians will *never* have to face—separation from Jesus' unfailing Love.

We followers of Jesus face a glorious challenge every single day: to trust in His Love regardless of our circumstances. We will experience many losses over the years, but the one thing we cannot live without is the one thing we can never lose—Jesus' loving Presence. Even this great truth, however, may not be enough to carry us confidently through our toughest times, unless it is accompanied by experiential knowledge of Jesus.

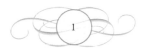

We must search for and "see" His Love in the moments of our lives.

Jesus Lives: Seeing His Love in Your Life is designed to help you encounter your living Savior as you walk through the various circumstances of your days—and especially as you deal with difficulties. I wrote this book with a focus on God's astonishing Love for His children. As with my previous books, I composed this one by listening and writing, listening and writing—always in prayerful dependence on the Holy Spirit. I wrote down what I "heard" from the Lover of my soul while listening intently in His Presence. *Jesus Lives* is written in the same style as *Jesus Calling*: from the perspective of Jesus speaking to *you*.

During the writing of this book my health steadily deteriorated until I was weaker than ever before. As a result, awareness of my neediness reached an all-time high, and the process of writing became more than ever an act of faith. I looked to the Lord in His infinite sufficiency—bringing Him only my utter insufficiency. Time after time He stooped down to help me, undeterred by how little I brought to the table. Sometimes He surprised me with the ardor of His Love. As I focused on Jesus, His compassionate Presence always encouraged me.

The Bible is the only infallible Word of God. My writings are based on that unchanging standard, and I try to ensure that they are consistent with biblical truth.

I encourage you to read the devotions in *Jesus Lives* slowly and prayerfully, opening your mind and heart to the One who loves you more than you can imagine. I hope you will also ponder the Bible verses I included with each entry. God's Word is alive and full of power; it penetrates the human heart deeply, and it changes lives.

I pray that God will use *Jesus Lives* to increase your awareness of Christ's Love in your life. I consider it a delightful privilege to pray for all readers of my books, and I make this a top priority each morning.

May you experience deeper, richer, more continual intimacy and communion with Jesus day by day.

Bountiful blessings!

Sarah Young

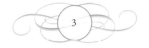

HIS LOVE

THE VERY NAME I USE TO ADDRESS YOU—
BELOVED—PROCLAIMS HOW DEARLY I LOVE
YOU. I showed you the *full extent of My Love* by enduring humiliation, torture, and death for you. No greater
love than this is possible, or even conceivable.

You have tucked into your memory many experiences of My unparalleled Love. I want you to dwell on
these memories: Enjoy them over and over again! This
practice will help convince your doubting heart that
My extraordinary Love is really yours—every nanosecond of this life and throughout eternity.

When you abide in Me, you also abide in My Love,
for *I am Love*. As you live close to Me—communing
with Me more and more—My living Presence permeates your entire being. This empowers you to *trust in
My unfailing Love*, secure in the salvation I won for you.

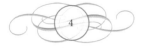

*It was just before the Passover Feast. Jesus knew that
the time had come for him to leave this world and go to
the Father. Having loved his own who were in the world,
he now showed them the full extent of his love.*
JOHN 13:1

*Greater love has no one than this, than
to lay down one's life for his friends.*
JOHN 15:13 NKJV

*We have come to know and have believed the love
which God has for us. God is love, and the one who
abides in love abides in God, and God abides in him.*
1 JOHN 4:16 NASB

*But I trust in your unfailing love;
my heart rejoices in your salvation.*
PSALM 13:5

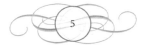

JOY

REJOICE IN ME ALWAYS. This is a moment-by-moment choice. It is possible to find Joy in Me even during the most difficult times. Because I am always near, I am constantly available to help you. I can even carry you through times of extreme adversity.

Imagine a woman who has become engaged to a man she deeply loves and admires. Her heart overflows with pleasure whenever she thinks about her beloved. Problems fade into the background, unable to dampen her enthusiasm and excitement. Similarly, when you remember that I am your perfect Betrothed and that you are promised to Me forever, you can rejoice in Me even though you face many problems.

It is in the present moment that you find Me ever near you. *My Presence in the present* is an endless source of Joy: *a continual feast!* The soul-satisfaction you find in Me helps you relate well to other people. As you enjoy My abiding Presence, you can bless others with *your gentleness*.

*Rejoice in the Lord always. I will say it again: Rejoice!
Let your gentleness be evident to all. The Lord is near.*
PHILIPPIANS 4:4–5

*All the days of the afflicted are evil, but he who is of a
merry heart has a continual feast.*
PROVERBS 15:15 NKJV

*My soul will be satisfied as with the richest of foods;
with singing lips my mouth will praise you.*
PSALM 63:5

*Abide in Me, and I in you. As the branch cannot
bear fruit of itself, unless it abides in the vine,
neither can you, unless you abide in Me.*
JOHN 15:4 NKJV

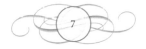

FAITH

MY LIGHT SHINES ON YOU CONTINUALLY, WHETHER YOU ARE AWARE OF IT OR NOT. During the *wee hours* of the night, your thoughts are often distorted—even catastrophic. Although you may feel as if you're enveloped in darkness, remember that *darkness and light are alike to Me.* I am with you, and My Love for you never fails. You need the Light of My Presence supremely more than you need the light of day.

When the way before you seems dark and threatening, you can still trust Me to guide you. *Walking by faith* is akin to using radar to discern the way you should go. Instead of trying to see through clouds of uncertainty up ahead, *fix your eyes on Me.* I can show you a way forward where there appears to be none. Moreover, as you strive to stay in communication with Me, your soul opens up to Me. Even in the midst of your struggle, My loving Presence can fill your soul with warm delight.

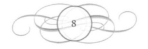

Even the darkness is not dark to You, And the night is as bright as the day. Darkness and light are alike to You.
PSALM 139:12 NASB

For we walk by faith, not by sight.
2 CORINTHIANS 5:7 NKJV

Let the morning bring me word of your unfailing love, for I have put my trust in you. Show me the way I should go, for to you I lift up my soul.
PSALM 143:8

Let us fix our eyes on Jesus, the author and perfecter of our faith, who for the joy set before him endured the cross, scorning its shame, and sat down at the right hand of the throne of God.
HEBREWS 12:2

ATTITUDE

IN MY PRESENCE YOU HAVE INFINITE APPROVAL. You often judge yourself on the basis of what you see in the mirror, even though you know how fickle and shallow that ever-changing image is. You tend to be equally enslaved to viewing yourself through the eyes of other people, rigorously evaluating your personal performance and almost always feeling displeased with something you've said or done.

"Enslaved" is an appropriate word. You are indeed a slave when you try to measure yourself through any perspective but Mine. Evaluating your worth based on how you look, to yourself or to others, is always a trap. It's as if you are sifting sand in a search for gold— looking only at the grains of sand filtering through the sieve, while ignoring the priceless nuggets that remain. The gold represents the eternal part of you: your soul. It is invisible to everyone but Me, the One who plans to spend eternity with you. Though invisible, a well-nurtured soul can actually improve your appearance: As you rest in the certainty of *My unfailing Love*, your face glows with *the Joy of My Presence*.

My approval of you is infinite because it will continue forever. It is based entirely on My righteousness,

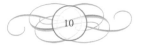

which is yours for all eternity. When you look in a mirror, try to see yourself as you truly are—arrayed in perfect righteousness, adorned in glowing approval.

Satisfy us in the morning with your unfailing love, that we may sing for joy and be glad all our days.

PSALM 90:14

Surely you have granted him eternal blessings and made him glad with the joy of your presence.

PSALM 21:6

I delight greatly in the LORD; my soul rejoices in my God. For he has clothed me with garments of salvation and arrayed me in a robe of righteousness, as a bridegroom adorns his head like a priest, and as a bride adorns herself with her jewels.

ISAIAH 61:10

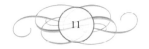

TRIALS

COME TO ME WITH THE DIFFICULTIES THAT ARE WEIGHING YOU DOWN. Even though there is no relief in sight, your troubles are actually *light and momentary*—from an eternal perspective. Your problems feel so heavy because you have given them too much power. Each time you focus on them and forget about Me, you empower them a bit more. Even small objects placed very close to your eyes can obscure most of the vista before you. I want you to put your troubles down long enough to view the vast expanse of Life that is spread out before you—all the way into eternity!

The best way to lay your problems down is: Bring them to Me. Unburden yourself by *pouring out your heart to Me*, for *I am your Refuge*. As you release your woes to Me (even temporarily), your vision improves and you can see Me more clearly. Linger with Me while My Light shines powerfully into your heart. This Light illuminates *the knowledge of the Majesty and Glory* revealed in My Face. *This* is the eternal Glory that outweighs all your troubles.

*Our light and momentary troubles are achieving for us
an eternal glory that far outweighs them all.*
2 CORINTHIANS 4:17

*Trust in him at all times, O people; pour out your
hearts to him, for God is our refuge. Selah.*
PSALM 62:8

*For God Who said, Let light shine out of darkness, has
shone in our hearts so as [to beam forth] the Light for
the illumination of the knowledge of the majesty and
glory of God [as it is manifest in the Person and is
revealed] in the face of Jesus Christ (the Messiah).*
2 CORINTHIANS 4:6 AMP

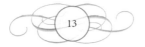

WORSHIP

I AM THE FIRM FOUNDATION ON WHICH YOU CAN DANCE AND SING PRAISES AND CONTINU-ALLY CELEBRATE MY PRESENCE—JUST AS YOU LONG TO. Most of the time, however, you feel earth-bound and weighed down. Worshiping Me requires the engagement of your entire being—something you delight in and yet somehow resist.

If you want to learn how to celebrate Me more consistently, more abundantly, begin by lingering in My peaceful Presence. As you relax in *My everlasting arms*, sense how safe and secure you are. I am indeed the rock-solid Foundation on which you can live exu-berantly. Dancing, singing, and praying are ways you can express your delight in Me.

My very Presence radiates Joy in vast, unmeasured fullness! When you praise Me, your Joy increases, as does your awareness of My holy Presence. Your body may or may not be mightily engaged in this endeavor, but *I see into your heart*. That is where the ultimate celebration of My Presence takes place.

The eternal God is your refuge,
and underneath are the everlasting arms.
DEUTERONOMY 33:27

You have made known to me the path of life; you
will fill me with joy in your presence, with eternal
pleasures at your right hand.
PSALM 16:11

David, wearing a linen ephod, danced
before the LORD with all his might.
2 SAMUEL 6:14

But the LORD said to Samuel, "Do not look at his
appearance or at his physical stature, because I have
refused him. For the LORD does not see as man sees;
for man looks at the outward appearance,
but the LORD looks at the heart."
1 SAMUEL 16:7 NKJV

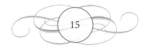

TRUST

I WANT TO MAKE YOUR LIFE A GLORIOUS ADVENTURE, BUT YOU MUST STOP STRIVING FOR A LIFESTYLE THAT FEELS SAFE. I know how ambivalent your heart is in all of this: You long for the adventure that a life abandoned to Me can be, and at the same time, you cling to old ways because change frightens you. Though you feel safest when your life is predictable and things seem to be under control, I want you to break free and discover the adventures I have planned for you.

The greatest adventure of all is knowing Me abundantly: discovering *how wide and long and high and deep* is My Love for you. The power of My vast Love can feel overwhelming. That is why many people choose to limit their knowledge of Me, keeping Me at a distance. How this grieves Me! People settle for mediocrity because it feels more comfortable. Meanwhile, they continue to battle fear. Only My Love is strong enough to break the hold that fear has on you. A predictable lifestyle may feel safer, but it can shield you from what you need most of all—Me!

When unexpected events shake up your routines, rejoice. This is exactly what you need, to wake

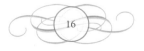

you up and point you toward Me. Recognize that you are on the threshold of a new adventure, and that I will be with you each step of the way. As we venture out together, cling tightly to My hand. The more you abandon yourself to Me, the more exuberantly you can experience My Love.

And I pray that you, being rooted and established in love, may have power, together with all the saints, to grasp how wide and long and high and deep is the love of Christ.
EPHESIANS 3:17–18

There is no fear in love. But perfect love drives out fear, because fear has to do with punishment. The one who fears is not made perfect in love.
1 JOHN 4:18

My soul clings to you; your right hand upholds me.
PSALM 63:8

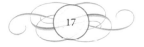

DEPENDING ON HIM

YOUR AWARENESS OF YOUR DEEP NEED FOR
ME IS A PROFOUND STRENGTH. People who think
they don't need Me are in serious trouble, because they
rely on their own insufficient abilities. I am training
you to depend on Me—*your Strength.*

Living in a fallen world can weigh you down.
However, as you keep looking to Me, *I make your feet
like the feet of a deer.* I lighten your load so much that
you hardly notice the jagged rocks beneath your feet or
the steepness of your ascent. Before you know it, you
are on the high places—with Me!

You need to remember that I am Sovereign. I will
not help you go along a path that is not My choice for
you. So it's vital to *commit your way to Me,* asking Me
to lead you each step of the way. *This* is how you collaborate with Me as *I enable you to go on the heights.*

The Sovereign LORD is my strength; he makes my feet
like the feet of a deer, he enables me to go on the heights.
HABAKKUK 3:19

Though youths grow weary and tired,
And vigorous young men stumble badly,
Yet those who wait for the LORD will gain new strength;
They will mount up with wings like eagles,
They will run and not get tired,
They will walk and not become weary.
ISAIAH 40:30–31 NASB

Commit your way to the LORD, trust also in Him,
and He shall bring it to pass.
PSALM 37:5 NKJV

HOPE

I AM TRAINING YOU TO HOLD IN YOUR HEART A DUAL FOCUS: MY CONTINUAL PRESENCE AND THE HOPE OF HEAVEN. You'll find no deeper comfort than knowing *I am with you always*, both here on earth and throughout eternity in heaven. You have known this great truth in your head for many years. However, your heart is fickle and tends to chase after other gods. Only as My Spirit helps you can you grasp the awesomeness of My Presence with you forever. I am indeed with you—watching over you wherever you are, wherever you go. Simply accept My Presence with you as reality: the deepest Reality. Build your life on this absolute truth, which is like *building your house on a rock*.

Your heart and mind *will* wander away from Me, but My Spirit within can remind you to return. You need only to ask the Holy Spirit to help you in this way. He delights in being your *Helper*.

Rejoice, for I am with you not only in this life but in the life to come. Let the promise of heaven flood your heart with My eternal Presence!

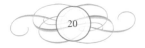

I am with you and will watch over you wherever you go.
GENESIS 28:15

Therefore everyone who hears these words of
mine and puts them into practice is like a wise
man who built his house on the rock.
MATTHEW 7:24

I will ask the Father, and He will give you another Helper,
that He may be with you forever; that is the Spirit of truth,
whom the world cannot receive, because it does not see
Him or know Him, but you know Him because
He abides with you and will be in you.
JOHN 14:16–17 NASB

In my Father's house are many rooms; if it were not so,
I would have told you. I am going there to prepare a
place for you. And if I go and prepare a place for you,
I will come back and take you to be with me
that you also may be where I am.
JOHN 14:2–3

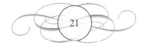

21

BROKENNESS

YOUR WEAKNESS AND BROKENNESS DRAW ME EVER SO NEAR YOU. You can open up to Me because I understand you perfectly. My compassion for you is overflowing. As you open yourself to My healing Presence, I fill you with *Peace that transcends understanding.* So stop trying to figure everything out. Instead, lean on Me, letting your head rest on My chest. While you rest, I will be watching over you and all that concerns you.

Trust Me in the depths of your being, where I live in union with you. My healing work in you is most effective when you are actively trusting Me. *Though the mountains be shaken and the hills be removed, yet My unfailing Love for you will not be shaken.* This is the essence of My compassion for you: No matter how desperate your circumstances, the one thing you can always count on is *My unfailing Love.*

A bruised reed he will not break,
and a smoldering wick he will not snuff out.

ISAIAH 42:3

Do not be anxious about anything, but in everything,
by prayer and petition, with thanksgiving, present
your requests to God. And the peace of God, which
transcends all understanding, will guard your hearts
and your minds in Christ Jesus.

PHILIPPIANS 4:6–7

Lean on, trust in, and be confident in the Lord
with all your heart and mind and do not rely on
your own insight or understanding.

PROVERBS 3:5 AMP

"Though the mountains be shaken and the hills be
removed, yet my unfailing love for you will not be
shaken nor my covenant of peace be removed,"
says the LORD, who has compassion on you.

ISAIAH 54:10

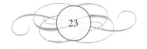

IDOLATRY

EVER SINCE THE FALL, PEOPLE HAVE WANTED TO MAKE IDOLS OF THEMSELVES AND THEIR OWN CREATIONS. They find it easier to deify something visible than to worship My unseen Reality. You have spent years trying to perfect yourself. Now you are more vulnerable to idolizing what you have made or done than what you are. This is a rather subtle sin, especially when you have created something for My Glory and purposes. I have deigned to use some of your creations to bless other people, and this has delighted you. When they express their appreciation to you, you soak up their praises. You forget that everything you make is as flawed as you are. Just as you are a *jar of clay* filled with heavenly contents, so are the things you have made or done for Me.

I am *Christ in you*—shining *the Light of the knowledge of My Glory* into your heart. I am the Treasure that fills not only you but also your creations of clay, giving them meaning. When you do your work in dependence on Me, I can use it powerfully for My purposes. Delight in what we accomplish together, but find your utmost

Joy in Me—your eternal Treasure. As you gaze at Me in loving worship, rejoice that your name is written in heaven's book of Life.

For it is the God who commanded light to shine out of darkness, who has shone in our hearts to give the light of the knowledge of the glory of God in the face of Jesus Christ. But we have this treasure in jars of clay, to show that this all-surpassing power is from God and not from us.
2 CORINTHIANS 4:6–7

To them God has chosen to make known among the Gentiles the glorious riches of this mystery, which is Christ in you, the hope of glory.
COLOSSIANS 1:27

However, do not rejoice that the spirits submit to you, but rejoice that your names are written in heaven.
LUKE 10:20

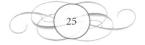

ASSURANCE

I KNOW FULL WELL THE THOUGHTS AND ATTITUDES OF YOUR HEART, SO IT IS WISE TO BE HONEST WITH ME. When your heart overflows with Love and Joy, I rejoice with you and delight in you. When you are rebellious and ungrateful, I continue to love you perfectly—even though your behavior is unacceptable. The more you believe in Me—who I am and what I have done—the better your attitude will be.

When you are feeling ungrateful, you need to focus on *the goal of your faith: the salvation of your soul.* No matter what you suffer in this life, your soul is absolutely secure. You have an eternity of inexpressibly wondrous Life reserved for you in heaven. This glorious inheritance has been credited to your account ever since you trusted Me as your Savior-God. As you ponder the wonders of your soul's salvation, you become free—free to receive Joy beyond description and full of Glory!

For the word of God is living and active. Sharper
than any double-edged sword, it penetrates even to
dividing soul and spirit, joints and marrow; it
judges the thoughts and attitudes of the heart.

HEBREWS 4:12

Though you have not seen him, you love him;
and even though you do not see him now, you believe
in him and are filled with an inexpressible and
glorious joy, for you are receiving the goal of
your faith, the salvation of your souls.

1 PETER 1:8–9

Give thanks to the LORD, for he is good;
his love endures forever.

PSALM 107:1

I give them eternal life, and they shall never perish;
no one can snatch them out of my hand.

JOHN 10:28

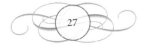

FEAR

FEARFULNESS IS A FORM OF BONDAGE. I died on the cross for you so that you would not be a slave to fear. When I see My children continuing to live in *bondage to fear,* I am grieved. My sacrifice was not only to provide forgiveness of sins but also to open the way to My Father's heart. Now that you trust Me as Savior, you are the recipient of *perfect Love*—My Love, Abba's Love. This *perfect Love drives out fear, because fear has to do with punishment* (and there is no punishment for My followers).

People are born into the world in spiritual bondage, including bondage to fear. Because you inhabit both a fallen world and a fallen body, it isn't easy to break free from fearfulness. However, *the Spirit of adoption* can help you in this struggle, enabling you to see yourself as you truly are: a much-loved child of God! The Spirit frees you to *cry out, "Abba, Father,"* believing you are His precious, adopted child. In the presence of a loving, strong father even the most frightened child eventually calms down. You have a perfectly loving, infinitely strong Father, so bring your fears freely to Him. Let Him hold you close to His Abba-heart, where you know you are safe. Open your heart to receive vast

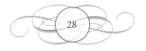

quantities of His Love. The more of this Love you hold in your heart, the less room there is for fear. Receive Our Love in full measure!

*For you did not receive the spirit of bondage
again to fear, but you received the Spirit of adoption
by whom we cry out, "Abba, Father."*
ROMANS 8:15

*There is no fear in love. But perfect love drives out fear,
because fear has to do with punishment.*
1 JOHN 4:18

*Now the Lord is the Spirit, and where the
Spirit of the Lord is, there is freedom.*
2 CORINTHIANS 3:17

*"As the Father has loved me, so have I loved you.
Now remain in my love."*
JOHN 15:9

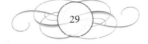

GRACE

MY GRACE IS SUFFICIENT FOR YOU, BUT ITS SUFFICIENCY IS FOR ONE DAY AT A TIME. That's why it is essential for you to learn how to live in the present.

Your mind so easily slips into the future, where worries abound. You also spend way too much time analyzing the past. Meanwhile, splendors of the present moment parade before you, and you don't even notice. Part of the problem is your tendency to strive for self-sufficiency. I will help you learn to rest in *My* sufficiency, depending on Me more and more.

You need My grace in order to live in the present. Grace is all about My provision for you, but accepting that goes against the grain of your natural tendencies. Each day you face a number of situations requiring My help. Moment by moment I proffer to you the needed assistance. Your part is to recognize your neediness and receive what I offer.

My Presence is with you always, providing everything you need. So *don't worry about tomorrow's needs.* My sufficiency is for a day at a time—today!

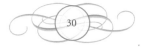

But he said to me, "My grace is sufficient for you,
for my power is made perfect in weakness." Therefore
I will boast all the more gladly about my weaknesses,
so that Christ's power may rest on me.

2 CORINTHIANS 12:9

Those who look to him are radiant;
their faces are never covered with shame.

PSALM 34:5

And my God will meet all your needs
according to his glorious riches in Christ Jesus.

PHILIPPIANS 4:19

Therefore do not worry about tomorrow,
for tomorrow will worry about itself. Each day
has enough trouble of its own.

MATTHEW 6:34

SORROW

TRUST IN ME AT ALL TIMES. I know the pain and sorrow you are feeling, and I want you to *pour out your heart* in My Presence. You need to release all those emotions in a safe place. Demonstrate your trust in Me by opening your heart to Me; as you do so, I promise to keep you safe.

Remember that I am a *Man of sorrows, fully acquainted with grief.* Because of all I suffered, I can empathize with you and share your pain. As you pour out your emotions in My Presence, your heavy burden grows lighter. You no longer carry your sorrows alone. You release them to Me, and I then *relieve and refresh your soul.* Moreover, as your heavy heart grows lighter, you are freed to learn more of Me: who I really am.

Come to Me and get to know Me in ever-increasing depth and breadth. You will find that I am indeed a Refuge—a safe place flooded with eternal Love. Linger a while in My Presence, letting My Love soak into your soul.

*Trust in Him at all times, you people; pour out
your heart before Him; God is a refuge for us.*
PSALM 62:8 NKJV

*Fear of man will prove to be a snare,
but whoever trusts in the LORD is kept safe.*
PROVERBS 29:25

*He was despised and forsaken of men,
A man of sorrows and acquainted with grief;
And like one from whom men hide their face
He was despised, and we did not esteem Him.*
ISAIAH 53:3 NASB

*Come to Me, all you who labor and are heavy-laden
and overburdened, and I will cause you to rest.
[I will ease and relieve and refresh your souls.]*
MATTHEW 11:28 AMP

33

ABIDING IN HIM

INVITE ME INTO YOUR THOUGHTS BY
WHISPERING MY NAME; SUDDENLY YOUR DAY
BRIGHTENS AND FEELS MORE USER-FRIENDLY.
When you speak My Name in loving trust, you sense
My Presence and feel yourself drawing closer to Me.

There is great Power in My Name: Simply whispering "Jesus" can turn a hard day into a good one. By
calling on My Name frequently, you acknowledge your
continual need of Me. And when you pray My Name,
you are actually calling upon My very Being. I joyfully
respond to your invitation by *coming nearer to you.*

I am pleased by your desire to rely on Me in ordinary moments as well as in the big events of your life.
When you whisper My Name, I respond not only to
your neediness but also to your love. As you look to
Me, *My Face shines upon you* in radiant approval—
brightening your day and helping you feel secure.

Salvation is found in no one else,
for there is no other name under heaven given
to men by which we must be saved.
ACTS 4:12

Come near to God and he will come near to you.
JAMES 4:8

And everyone who calls on the
name of the Lord will be saved.
ACTS 2:21

The Lord make His face to shine upon and
enlighten you and be gracious (kind, merciful, and
giving favor) to you. The Lord lift up His [approving]
countenance upon you and give you peace
(tranquility of heart and life continually).
NUMBERS 6:25–26 AMP

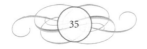

STRIVING

INSTEAD OF RUSHING TO PURSUE A GOAL, TAKE TIME TO TALK WITH ME ABOUT IT. I realize that striving to achieve comes almost as naturally to you as breathing. When a goal grabs your attention, your instinct is to "go for it" without really thinking it through. You may invest a lot of time and energy in the endeavor—only later realizing that it was the wrong pursuit. But when you take the time to first discuss matters with Me, you experience much more satisfaction.

There are many benefits to talking with Me—before, during, and after your quest. *The Light of My Presence* illuminates the pursuit so you can see it from My perspective. As your perspective lines up more with Mine, you gain a growing desire to please Me. This desire produces benefits far beyond the task at hand: It deepens your relationship with Me.

If you discern that your pursuit accords with My will, then you can go forward confidently. As you work collaboratively with Me, continue to communicate about what you are doing. When your goal has been achieved, thank Me for My help and guidance. Rejoice in what we have accomplished together!

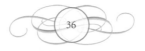

Blessed are those who have learned to acclaim you,
who walk in the light of your presence, O Lord.
They rejoice in your name all day long;
they exult in your righteousness.

PSALM 89:15–16

There are many plans in a man's heart,
nevertheless the Lord's counsel—that will stand.

PROVERBS 19:21 NKJV

Commit your way to the Lord,
trust also in Him, and He will do it.

PSALM 37:5 NASB

I can do all things through Him who strengthens me.

PHILIPPIANS 4:13 NASB

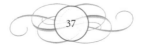

HIS SUFFICIENCY

I OFFER YOU GODLY CONTENTMENT: A STATE OF SERENITY THAT FLOWS OUT OF TRUSTING IN MY GREAT SUFFICIENCY. I am teaching you to depend on Me alone—content with whatever I provide. Relying solely on Me is a way of rich blessing, even though it may lead you along paths you would not have chosen. If you are truly content to live with My provisions for you—now and in the future—you will not be plagued by anxiety. Instead of worrying about "what ifs" *your heart will be firmly fixed—confident in Me.*

I realize this world is full of fear-inducing messages. Daily news reports can fill your mind with fearful thoughts. Advertisers intentionally stimulate anxiety and insecurity, so they can demonstrate how their products will help you—making you happy and secure. To counteract these harmful messages, it's essential for you to exert some control over your thinking. Ask the Holy Spirit to help you think My thoughts. The more He controls your mind, the more you will experience *Life and Peace.*

Remember that *you brought nothing into the world:* Everything you have is a gift from Me, including each

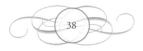

breath you breathe. Though *you can carry nothing out* of this world, the spiritual transformation I am working in you is eternal. Collaborate with Me as I transform you into My likeness, preparing you for the ultimate in blissful contentment—heaven!

Now godliness with contentment is great gain.
For we brought nothing into this world, and it is
certain we can carry nothing out.
1 TIMOTHY 6:6–7 NKJV

He shall not be afraid of evil tidings;
his heart is firmly fixed, trusting (leaning on
and being confident) in the Lord.
PSALM 112:7 AMP

The mind of sinful man is death, but the mind
controlled by the Spirit is life and peace.
ROMANS 8:6

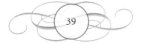

ADVERSITY

NO MATTER WHAT HARDSHIPS THE WORLD MAY THROW AT YOU, YOU HAVE—IN ME— EVERYTHING YOU NEED TO PERSEVERE. Despair is a deep pit, and sometimes you totter around its edges, precariously close to falling in. Your only hope at such times is to *fix your eyes on Me*. The more perplexed you are—bewildered by complex circumstances—the easier it is to lose your balance. To keep from falling, you must change your focus: from your circumstances to My Presence. This requires strenuous effort on your part, because you have not fully accepted the limitations of your mind. Your natural tendency is to keep thinking about a difficult situation *ad nauseam*—trying to figure it out. However, I am always nearby, eager to help you change your focus time after time.

Though you may be *hard pressed on every side*, you need not be crushed by your difficulties. You are not alone in your battles because I will never, ever abandon you. Even if you are struck down by a fatal blow, you will not be destroyed. I am *the Shepherd and Guardian of your soul*—the part of you that is indestructible. *I give you eternal Life, and you will never perish. No one can snatch you out of My hand!*

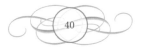

We are hard pressed on every side, but not crushed;
perplexed, but not in despair; persecuted, but not
abandoned; struck down, but not destroyed.

2 CORINTHIANS 4:8

Let us fix our eyes on Jesus, the author and perfecter
of our faith, who for the joy set before him endured
the cross, scorning its shame, and sat down at the
right hand of the throne of God.

HEBREWS 12:2

For you were continually straying like sheep,
but now you have returned to the Shepherd
and Guardian of your souls.

1 PETER 2:25 NASB

I give them eternal life, and they shall never perish;
no one can snatch them out of my hand.

JOHN 10:28

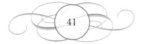

41

INTIMACY WITH HIM

YOU HAVE THE AMAZING PRIVILEGE OF KNOWING ME INTIMATELY, YET THIS PRIVILEGE IS NOT AN INVITATION TO ACT AS IF YOU WERE MY EQUAL. I want you to worship Me as *King of kings* while walking hand in hand with Me.

I know it's not easy for you to strike that balance. I took a huge risk when I created mankind in My own image. I made you with the awesome ability to reverence and love Me freely, without coercion. I paid enormously for your freedom—with My own blood. This payment has made it possible for you to know Me, *the King of kings and Lord of lords*. When one of My children draws near Me in reverent awe, I open My heart and offer intimate friendship. The Joy we share in one another cannot be measured.

However, from time to time you overstep your bounds, forgetting who I AM. You talk to Me carelessly, even slanderously. While our intimacy is hindered by your irreverent attitude, My Love for you is constant. When you remember My majestic Presence and return to Me repentantly, I not only forgive you, but I rush to meet you and enfold you in My embrace. I celebrate with you the Joy of being close again as we walk together down *the path of Life*.

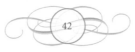

Until the appearing of our Lord Jesus Christ, which God will bring about in his own time—God, the blessed and only Ruler, the King of kings and Lord of lords.

1 TIMOTHY 6:14–15

Jesus said to them, "Most assuredly, I say to you, before Abraham was, I AM."

JOHN 8:58 NKJV

So he got up and went to his father. But while he was still a long way off, his father saw him and was filled with compassion for him; he ran to his son, threw his arms around him and kissed him.

LUKE 15:20

You have made known to me the path of life; you will fill me with joy in your presence, with eternal pleasures at your right hand.

PSALM 16:11

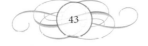

BROKENNESS

YOU ARE FEELING BROKENHEARTED AND BOUND: ENTANGLED IN WEBS OF DISCOURAGEMENT. Pick up the pieces of your broken heart—scattered all around you—and bring them to Me. Place them on the white linen cloth I provide, and wait in My healing Presence. Sit still in My holy Light while I cleanse you from binding webs of discouragement. Look into My Face and see the great Love I have for you. Because My Love is limitless, I never run out of compassion. When you feel on the brink of giving up, remind yourself of My great faithfulness: I never give up on you!

Though your disappointment is real, My Presence with you is *even more real*. Stay close to Me as I work on mending your broken heart. Of course, your repaired heart will not be exactly as it was before, but in some ways it will be much better. Your renewed heart— stripped of its cherished hopes—will have more space for Me.

"The Spirit of the Lord . . . has sent Me to heal the
brokenhearted, to proclaim liberty to the captives, and
the opening of the prison to those who are bound."

ISAIAH 61:1 NKJV

As the eyes of slaves look to the hand of their master,
as the eyes of a maid look to the hand of her mistress,
so our eyes look to the LORD our God,
till he shows us his mercy.

PSALM 123:2

Because of the LORD's great love we are not consumed,
for his compassions never fail. They are new
every morning; great is your faithfulness.

LAMENTATIONS 3:22–23

Create in me a clean heart, O God,
and renew a steadfast spirit within me.

PSALM 51:10 NKJV

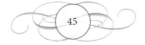

DESIRING HIM

I AM PLEASED WITH YOU, MY CHILD. Though you are still a *work in progress*, you desire for Me to sanctify you—to make you holy. My *sacrifice for sins* made you eternally perfect the instant you trusted Me as Savior. This sacrifice was perfect because *I* am perfect and I am your Substitute in the courts of heaven. However, as long as you live in this world, you inhabit the *not yet* of brokenness—in you and all around you. This explains the emptiness you often feel as you long for both your perfection in holiness and your perfect home in heaven.

The best way to enhance My sanctifying work in you is to love Me with *all your heart and mind— with your entire being and all your might*. King David expressed such ardor when he leapt and *danced before Me with all his might*. In spite of the serious sins he committed, he was a *man after My own heart*.

Instead of focusing on all the brokenness in and around you, fan the flames of your love for Me. Though this love may be like the flickering flame of a candle, My Love for you is like a blazing forest fire. Come more and more into My passionate Presence, and My holy Fire will ignite holy ardor in you.

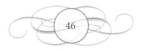

*But this Man, after He had offered one sacrifice for
sins forever, sat down at the right hand of God. . . .
For by one offering He has perfected forever
those who are being sanctified.*
HEBREWS 10:12–14 NKJV

*And you shall love the Lord your God with
all your [mind and] heart and with your
entire being and with all your might.*
DEUTERONOMY 6:5 AMP

*David, wearing a linen ephod,
danced before the LORD with all his might.*
2 SAMUEL 6:14

*After removing Saul, he made David their king.
He testified concerning him: "I have found David
son of Jesse a man after my own heart; he will
do everything I want him to do."*
ACTS 13:22

47

PRAYER

WHEN YOU FEEL UNABLE TO PRAY, REMEMBER THAT THE SPIRIT HIMSELF INTERCEDES FOR YOU WITH GROANS THAT WORDS CANNOT EXPRESS. Some of your prayers that you consider frantic and unintelligible are actually quite profound. They rise from the depths of your heart—all the way to heaven. To form these deep prayers, you need only turn toward Me with the concerns that lie heavy on your heart.

I want you to *watch in hope* as you *wait for Me, your Savior*. Wait expectantly: confident that I will do what is best. The longer you have to wait, the more you must rely on your trust in Me. If you start to feel anxious, seek My help with short prayers such as "Jesus, fill me with Your Peace." You may breathe these brief prayers as often as needed. As you put your hope in Me, *My unfailing Love rests peacefully upon you.*

*In the same way, the Spirit helps us in our weakness.
We do not know what we ought to pray for, but the
Spirit himself intercedes for us with groans that words
cannot express. And he who searches our hearts knows
the mind of the Spirit, because the Spirit intercedes
for the saints in accordance with God's will.*

ROMANS 8:26–27

*But as for me, I watch in hope for the LORD,
I wait for God my Savior; my God will hear me.*

MICAH 7:7

*We wait in hope for the LORD; he is our help and
our shield. In him our hearts rejoice, for we trust
in his holy name. May your unfailing love rest
upon us, O LORD, even as we put our hope in you.*

PSALM 33:20–22

HOPE

BE STEADFAST AND PATIENT IN SUFFERING. Affliction is a largely unappreciated gift among My children. Decades of "health and wealth" teaching have obscured the benefits of suffering. As a result, a secular worldview that despises pain and sorrow has infiltrated the church.

When painful circumstances are weighing you down, I encourage you to *rejoice and exult in hope:* to *leap joyously upward.* Although physical jumping is sometimes impossible or inappropriate, your soul can leap upward at any time. As you *lift your soul* to Me in hopeful anticipation, My showers of Joy fall upon and within you. The longer and more expectantly you wait in My Presence, the more abundantly I can bless you. One way to enhance this transaction is to lift your wide-open arms up toward Me—as if you were celebrating a triumphant moment in your life. This posture expresses exultant Joy, and I respond by filling your soul with *more* Joy. This puts you on an upward spiral of rejoicing. If you want to verbalize your jubilation, one of the best ways is to speak, sing, or shout: "Hallelujah!"

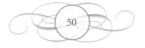

*Rejoice and exult in hope; be steadfast and patient in
suffering and tribulation; be constant in prayer.*
ROMANS 12:12 AMP

*May the God of hope fill you with all joy and
peace as you trust in him, so that you may overflow
with hope by the power of the Holy Spirit.*
ROMANS 15:13

*Rejoice the soul of Your servant, for to You,
O Lord, I lift up my soul.*
PSALM 86:4 NKJV

*After this I heard what sounded like the roar of a great
multitude in heaven shouting: "Hallelujah! Salvation
and glory and power belong to our God . . ."*
REVELATION 19:1

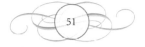

PLEASING HIM

A SUCCESSFUL DAY IS ONE IN WHICH YOU HAVE STAYED IN TOUCH WITH ME, EVEN IF MANY THINGS REMAIN UNDONE AT THE END OF THE DAY. It sounds almost too good to be true, doesn't it? You rarely reach day's end without a sense of failure to some degree. The various means and measures of worldly "success" pull on you constantly, leaving you in a fragmented, unfocused condition.

To avoid confusion, you need a rule of thumb: Seek to please Me. When communicating with Me is your highest priority, I am pleased. The more you commune with Me as you go through a day, the more you walk in My ways. The Light of My Presence illumines the path before you, making sin both obvious and abhorrent. This same Light *satisfies your soul*. So make this a successful day by staying in communication with Me.

Jesus replied: "'Love the Lord your God with all your heart and with all your soul and with all your mind.' This is the first and greatest commandment."

MATTHEW 22:37–38

You have set our iniquities before you, our secret sins in the light of your presence.

PSALM 90:8

This is what the LORD says: "Stand at the crossroads and look; ask for the ancient paths, ask where the good way is, and walk in it, and you will find rest for your souls."

JEREMIAH 6:16

My soul shall be satisfied as with marrow and fatness, And my mouth shall praise You with joyful lips.

PSALM 63:5 NKJV

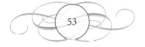

ENDURANCE

Keep your focus on Me—and on the crown of Life I have promised to those who love Me. There is a sense in which life on this earth is an endurance contest. It can be helpful to view your life this way, because then you're not shocked or disappointed by the many trials you encounter. Nonetheless, I do provide splashes of pleasure even in the midst of your hardest times. Among the many blessings I have for you, the Joy of My Presence is always available to you.

The crown of Life is similar to the wreath that was awarded for athletic victory in biblical times. However, those athletes competed to get a perishable crown—a wreath of greenery—and you are competing for *a crown that will last forever!* Whenever you are feeling battered by life's trials, remember *the crown of righteousness* that is stored up for you. Because it is *My* righteousness that saves you, this eternal reward is absolutely guaranteed. I have promised to give it to all those who love Me—who long for My return. When I, *the Chief Shepherd,* come back for you, *you will receive the crown of Glory that will never fade away!*

Blessed is the man who perseveres under trial, because when he has stood the test, he will receive the crown of life that God has promised to those who love him.
JAMES 1:12

Everyone who competes in the games goes into strict training. They do it to get a crown that will not last; but we do it to get a crown that will last forever.
1 CORINTHIANS 9:25

Finally, there is laid up for me the crown of righteousness, which the Lord, the righteous Judge, will give to me on that Day, and not to me only but also to all who have loved His appearing.
2 TIMOTHY 4:8 NKJV

And when the Chief Shepherd appears, you will receive the crown of glory that will never fade away.
1 PETER 5:4

THANKFULNESS

EVERY TIME YOU THANK ME, YOU ACKNOWL-
EDGE THAT I AM YOUR LORD AND PROVIDER.
And every time you receive with thanksgiving, you
demonstrate your kinship with Me.

Yet even though you are My child, and you know
you're supposed to *give thanks in all circumstances*, sometimes your words ring hollow: You can say them without
feeling the least bit thankful. It's especially hard for you
to be grateful in the midst of a bad day, when everything
seems to be going wrong.

I know what goes on in your heart far better than
you do. I know when you feel thankful, and when you
don't. However, I can also see in the depths of your heart
a desire to please Me by offering thanks even when you
don't feel like it.

When you struggle to be grateful, stop and remember who I AM: *the Author of your life* and your faith. You
are utterly dependent on Me for everything, including
your next breath. Every good gift is from Me! When you
thank Me during a difficult day, you are assuming the
proper stance for a child of God. If you persevere in this
thankfulness, resisting the temptation to grumble, you
can find Joy and Peace in the midst of your struggles.

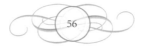

*Give thanks in all circumstances,
for this is God's will for you in Christ Jesus.*
1 THESSALONIANS 5:18

*You killed the author of life, but God raised him
from the dead. We are witnesses of this.*
ACTS 3:15

*Every good and perfect gift is from above,
coming down from the Father of the heavenly lights,
who does not change like shifting shadows.*
JAMES 1:17

*Therefore, since we are receiving a kingdom that
cannot be shaken, let us be thankful, and so worship
God acceptably with reverence and awe.*
HEBREWS 12:28

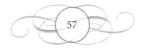

WEAKNESS

THANK ME FOR YOUR WEAKNESS. Even better, *boast gladly about your weaknesses*. Boasting can be either good or bad, depending on the object of the boast. People who brag about their wisdom, strength, or riches are offensive to Me. David was on the right track when he wrote about his soul *boasting in the Lord*. I want you to express pride in Me, just as the child of a good father likes to brag about his big, strong dad.

People who are well aware of their weaknesses are less tempted to boast about themselves. However, they are *more* vulnerable to other temptations: indulging in self-pity and complaints. So it is essential for weak ones to take pride in Me—rejoicing in who I Am.

Children tend to feel good about themselves when they are bragging about their fathers. Similarly, you can feel glad when you boast about Me: proudly *proclaiming My praises!* Awareness of your weaknesses has deepened your dependence on Me and helped you know Me more fully. So, you can be joyful about these afflictions that have blessed your relationship with Me. As you rejoice in your weaknesses, you open yourself to My Power. Let this sacred Power rest upon you, displaying My delight in you.

But He said to me, "My grace is sufficient for you,
for My power is made perfect in weakness." Therefore,
I will boast all the more gladly about my weaknesses,
so that Christ's power may rest upon me.

2 CORINTHIANS 12:9

This is what the LORD says: "Let not the wise man
boast of his wisdom or the strong man boast of
his strength or the rich man boast of his riches,
but let him who boasts boast about this:
that he understands and knows me."

JEREMIAH 9:23–24

My soul will boast in the LORD;
let the afflicted hear and rejoice.

PSALM 34:2

But you are a chosen generation, a royal priesthood,
a holy nation, His own special people, that you may
proclaim the praises of Him who called you out
of darkness into His marvelous light.

1 PETER 2:9 NKJV

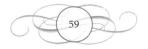

HIS LOVE

NOTHING CAN SEPARATE YOU FROM MY LOVE. When you trusted Me as Savior, I united Myself to you in eternal matrimony. Many things threaten to rip apart this holy bond—principalities and powers, controlling people, dire circumstances—but nothing can succeed, not even death. In fact, dying opens the way to ecstatic enjoyment of Me: exponentially better than your best moment on earth!

I embody not only perfect Love but *all the fullness of the Deity* as well. In Me you have everything you could ever need. Feelings of emptiness can serve as signals—reminding you to turn back toward Me. No matter what you are doing, I can be a co-participant with you. As you invite Me into more and more aspects of your life, you will discover a growing contentment within you. In times of adversity you can lean on Me for support; in joyous times you can celebrate with Me. I am as near as a whispered prayer—even nearer. *My banner over you is Love.*

*For I am persuaded that neither death nor life, nor
angels nor principalities nor powers, nor things present
nor things to come, nor height nor depth, nor any other
created thing, shall be able to separate us from the love
of God which is in Christ Jesus our Lord.*
ROMANS 8:38–39 NKJV

*The LORD is near to all who call on him,
to all who call on him in truth.*
PSALM 145:18

*For in Christ all the fullness of the Deity
lives in bodily form.*
COLOSSIANS 2:9

*He has taken me to the banquet hall,
and his banner over me is love.*
SONG OF SONGS 2:4

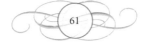

ABIDING IN HIM

I DELIGHT IN YOUR DESIRE TO LIVE STEAD-
FASTLY IN MY PRESENCE, AS IF YOU WERE A
TREE PLANTED CLOSE TO ME. However, unlike
a tree that cannot move from the place where it is
planted, each moment you can choose to stay near
Me—or not. Though I never leave you, you can "leave"
Me by forgetting I am with you. When that happens, you start looking for ways to bolster your own
resources. You also tend to run away from challenges I
have placed in your life.

My Spirit, who lives in you, will not leave you in
this compromised condition. He helps you remember
who you are and Whose you are. You belong to Me!
Returning to Me is not an arduous task. Simply affirm
your trust in *My unfailing Love*. As you thus reconnect with Me, My Love washes over you—cleansing,
refreshing, and filling you. No matter how many times
you forget Me, My Love for you will never fail. Grow
strong in this constant, nourishing Love.

*But I am like an olive tree, flourishing in the house of
God; I trust in God's unfailing love for ever and ever.*

PSALM 52:8

*Be strong and courageous. Do not be afraid or terrified
because of them, for the LORD your God goes with you;
he will never leave you nor forsake you.*

DEUTERONOMY 31:6

*In the same way, the Spirit helps us in our weakness.
We do not know what we ought to pray for,
but the Spirit himself intercedes for us with
groans that words cannot express.*

ROMANS 8:26

*To know the love of Christ which passes knowledge;
that you may be filled with all the fullness of God.*

EPHESIANS 3:19 NKJV

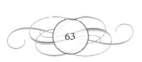

HIS PRESENCE

I AM IMMANUEL—GOD WITH YOU—AN EVER-PRESENT HELP IN TROUBLE. No matter what may happen, I am sufficient to provide whatever you need. Instead of imagining how you might respond to terrible things that could happen, draw your mind back to the present and take refuge in My Presence. I am much like a mother hen, eager to cover you with My protective pinions. As you snuggle *under My wings*, you will not only *find refuge*; you will also discover a growing ability to trust Me. It is in closeness to Me that you realize how trustworthy I am.

Remember that I am both *your Rock and your Redeemer*. Though I am impregnable in My vast strength, I became a vulnerable Man so I could redeem you from your sins. The more you take refuge in Me, the more aware you become of My overflowing Love. In Me you are utterly safe, for I am your Rock of everlasting Love!

God is our refuge and strength, an ever-present help in trouble. Therefore we will not fear, though the earth give way and the mountains fall into the heart of the sea.

PSALM 46:1–2

"O Jerusalem, Jerusalem, the one who kills the prophets and stones those who are sent to her! How often I wanted to gather your children together, as a hen gathers her chicks under her wings, but you were not willing!"

MATTHEW 23:37 NKJV

[Then] He will cover you with His pinions, and under His wings shall you trust and find refuge; His truth and His faithfulness are a shield and a buckler.

PSALM 91:4 AMP

May the words of my mouth and the meditation of my heart be pleasing in your sight, O LORD, my Rock and my Redeemer.

PSALM 19:14

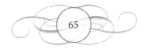

CONDEMNATION

I ASSURE YOU THERE IS NO CONDEMNATION
FOR THOSE WHO BELONG TO ME. You believe I
have freed you through My death on the cross for your
sins, yet you continue to struggle with feelings of condemnation. You long to experience the full liberation I
have made possible, and My Spirit can assist you with
this.

Ask the Holy Spirit to help you find freedom from
feelings of accusation. Acknowledge that those feelings have no basis in reality. Then look to Me through
eyes of faith. Delight yourself in My heavenly smile of
approval. The more you connect with Me by focusing
on My Presence, the more you can receive My loving
affirmation. The best antidote to feelings of condemnation is experiencing My Love for you.

You can also fight condemning feelings by pondering the truths of the gospel. The devil is *the father of
lies,* and he specializes in deception. Confront his hellish lies with biblical truth.

Finally, remember that My Spirit is *the Spirit of
Life.* Feelings of condemnation drain you of energy,
leaving you vulnerable. As My Spirit fills you with Life,
you are empowered to live abundantly—*to the full.*

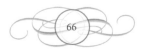

Therefore, there is now no condemnation
for those who are in Christ Jesus, because through
Christ Jesus the law of the Spirit of life set me
free from the law of sin and death.

ROMANS 8:1–2

By day the LORD directs his love,
at night his song is with me—
a prayer to the God of my life.

PSALM 42:8

He [the devil] was a murderer from the beginning,
not holding to the truth, for there is no truth in him.
When he lies, he speaks his native language,
for he is a liar and the father of lies.

JOHN 8:44

The thief comes only to steal and destroy; I have come
that they may have life, and have it to the full.

JOHN 10:10

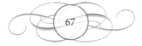

DEPENDING ON HIM

BEWARE OF DIVIDING UP YOUR LIFE INTO THINGS YOU CAN DO BY YOURSELF AND THINGS THAT REQUIRE MY HELP. The truth is, *everything* you do—even taking a breath—involves My assistance. *I sustain all things by My powerful Word.* So recognizing your utter dependence on Me builds a strong foundation on which you can do your work *heartily—from the soul.*

When you do routine tasks for Me, they gain meaning and even some sparkle. Your efforts become a way of expressing your love for Me. The more you love Me, the more you can enjoy doing tasks devoted to Me. I am less concerned about the outcome of your work than the attitude of your heart. When your deepest motive is to please Me, I deem your work *good.*

Your best efforts are those that emanate from your soul—where I live in intimate union with you. When you not only dedicate your efforts to Me but also keep looking to Me for help, your soul is fully engaged. You experience the thrill of seeing Me work through you. This collaborative way of doing things is effective and exciting; it is also deeply satisfying—to you *and* to Me.

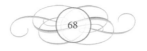

*The Son is the radiance of God's glory and
the exact representation of his being, sustaining
all things by his powerful word. After he had provided
purification for sins, he sat down at the right hand
of the Majesty in heaven.*

HEBREWS 1:3

*Whatever may be your task, work at it
heartily (from the soul), as [something done]
for the Lord and not for men.*

COLOSSIANS 3:23 AMP

*And we pray this in order that you may
live a life worthy of the Lord and may please him
in every way: bearing fruit in every good work,
growing in the knowledge of God.*

COLOSSIANS 1:10

*But be very careful to keep the commandment and
the law that Moses the servant of the LORD gave you:
to love the LORD your God, to walk in all his ways, to
obey his commands, to hold fast to him and to serve
him with all your heart and all your soul.*

JOSHUA 22:5

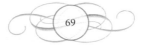

HEAVEN

MY KINGDOM CANNOT BE SHAKEN! This present world seems to be shaking more and more, leaving you off balance much of the time. As you worship Me, however, your perspective changes and you regain your balance. To worship Me *acceptably with reverence and awe*, thankfulness is essential. I designed you to *be thankful* on a daily, moment-by-moment basis. You need to resist the temptation to grumble when things don't go as you would like. Remember that I, your God, am *a consuming fire*. If you saw Me in all My Glory, you would be much too awestruck to venture even the tiniest complaint.

My unshakable kingdom is for all people who love Me, who know Me as Savior. This everlasting kingdom consists of things that *no eye has seen, no ear has heard, no mind has conceived*. I have prepared infinite, wondrous delights *for those who love Me*. Moreover, at the end of the age *I will come back and take you to be with Me so that you may be where I am*. Let these precious promises ignite your thankfulness, till you are aglow with My living Presence—shining brightly in this dark world.

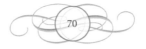

*Therefore, since we are receiving a kingdom
that cannot be shaken, let us be thankful, and so
worship God acceptably with reverence and awe,
for our God is a consuming fire.*
HEBREWS 12:28–29

*The sight of the glory of the LORD was like a
consuming fire on the top of the mountain
in the eyes of the children of Israel.*
EXODUS 24:17 NKJV

*However, as it is written: "No eye has seen, no ear
has heard, no mind has conceived what
God has prepared for those who love him."*
1 CORINTHIANS 2:9

*"And if I go and prepare a place for you,
I will come back and take you to be with
me that you also may be where I am."*
JOHN 14:3

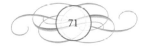

TRIALS

CONSIDER IT ALL JOY WHEN YOU ENCOUNTER
VARIOUS TRIALS. You can *consider* something a joyful opportunity even when you are feeling quite joyless.
Some definitions of "consider" are: "to think about
seriously; to regard as; to believe after deliberation."
You may need to ponder your circumstances at length
before you can view them in a positive light. You need
to give yourself time for your feelings to settle down.
It's hard to think clearly with high levels of emotions
surging through your brain. Once you have calmed
down, you will be able to think seriously about your
situation. Invite Me into this process of deliberation,
and My Presence will improve your perspective: helping you see your trials in the Light of eternity.

As you look at your circumstances from My perspective, you come to understand that these multiple problems
are *testing your faith*. This is both an opportunity (to
strengthen your faith) and a temptation (to let your feelings "trump" your faith).

One of the hardest things about trials is the uncertainty about how long they will last. Usually, you can't
predict or control the unpleasant circumstances. You
just have to live with them indefinitely. At times you

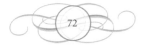

may feel as if you can endure no more, but you can always reach out to Me for help. As you cling to Me moment by moment, I enable you to persevere. This produces in you not only endurance but also *a harvest of righteousness and peace.*

Consider it all joy . . . when you encounter various trials, because you know that the testing of your faith develops perseverance.
JAMES 1:2–3

But Jesus looked at them and said to them, "With men this is impossible, but with God all things are possible."
MATTHEW 19:26 NKJV

No discipline seems pleasant at the time, but painful. Later on, however, it produces a harvest of righteousness and peace for those who have been trained by it.
HEBREWS 12:11

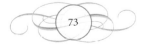

WORRY

Cast all your anxiety on Me. Unless you deal with it properly, anxiety can be toxic—both to you and to others. Simply releasing it is not sufficient. You need to project it vigorously away from yourself, toward Me. Consider the following illustration: If you accidentally pulled the pin out of a hand grenade, you would not hold onto the grenade or drop it near your feet. Nor would you pitch it to another person. You would throw it as far away as possible from yourself and others. When you *cast your anxiety on Me*, I remove it so far away that it cannot harm anyone. In fact, I delight in doing this very thing, because I *care for you* so compassionately.

Ever since the Fall, human emotions have been out of kilter. People often "act out" painful feelings without even realizing what is bothering them. Or they may bottle up their emotions and pretend everything is all right. I urge you to *be self-controlled and alert* so you can identify hurtful feelings and confess them to Me. Ask the Holy Spirit to help you with this. As you yield to His work within you, your anxious feelings will subside. My Spirit can accomplish holy changes in you—producing *Love, Joy, Peace . . . and self-control.*

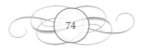

Cast all your anxiety on Him because He cares for you.
Be self-controlled and alert.
1 PETER 5:7–8

Shout for joy, O heavens; rejoice, O earth;
burst into song, O mountains!
For the LORD comforts his people and
will have compassion on his afflicted ones.
ISAIAH 49:13

You, however, are controlled not by the sinful nature
but by the Spirit, if the Spirit of God lives in you.
And if anyone does not have the Spirit of Christ,
he does not belong to Christ.
ROMANS 8:9

But the fruit of the Spirit is love, joy, peace,
longsuffering, kindness, goodness, faithfulness,
gentleness, self-control. Against such there is no law.
GALATIANS 5:22–23 NKJV

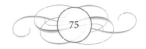

TRANSFORMATION

COME TO ME JUST AS YOU ARE. *I will give you a new heart and put a new spirit within you.* I am aware of the many little stones that mar the beauty of your heart. Trust Me to do what you are unable to do: remove the stony bits one by one. Do not expect this work in you to be painless. Heart surgery is serious, and it always involves pain. Many of the hard things you have experienced were, unknown to you, My skillful operations on your heart. When you are going through tough times, look up to Me with a wry smile and thank Me for the renewal I am working within you. This act of faith does not instantly stop your suffering, but it does lend meaning to your pain.

Marvel at the wonder of being *a new creation, grafted into Me—the Messiah.* You are forever set free from the condemning *law of sin and death.* You can rejoice in this glorious truth even while you are in the throes of suffering. Since I am the Creator of all that is, and you are made in My image, you have a wealth of creative powers within you. Strive to look at your circumstances from a fresh perspective: eager to collaborate with Me as I create newness within you—and through you. Though I am Lord of the universe, I

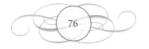

desire to work in partnership with you. As you say yes to this sacred adventure, you become more fully the one I designed you to be.

"I will give you a new heart and put a new spirit within you; I will take the heart of stone out of your flesh and give you a heart of flesh."
EZEKIEL 36:26 NKJV

Therefore if any person is [ingrafted] in Christ (the Messiah) he is a new creation (a new creature altogether); the old [previous moral and spiritual condition] has passed away.
2 CORINTHIANS 5:17 AMP

Therefore, there is now no condemnation for those who are in Christ Jesus, because through Christ Jesus the law of the Spirit of life set me free from the law of sin and death.
ROMANS 8:1–2

In these last days he has spoken to us by his Son, whom he appointed heir of all things, and through whom he made the universe.
HEBREWS 1:2

HIS SUFFICIENCY

I UNDERSTAND YOU PERFECTLY AND LOVE YOU ETERNALLY. It is your soul I love, rather than your appearance or performance. Sometimes you are so dissatisfied with both of these that they become your focus. To break free from this self-preoccupation, relax in My loving Presence and let the Light of My Love soak into your entire being. Rest deeply while I massage your thoughts and feelings, helping you change your focus from yourself to Me. Remember that I created you to know Me: to enjoy Me and center your life in Me. *Cease striving and know that I am God.*

The world abounds with idols—things you turn to when you want to feel better about yourself: eating, entertainment, exercise, mastery of something or someone. However, none of these things can slake the thirst of your soul, which yearns for Me alone. Idolatrous substitutes may suppress your appetite for Me, mainly by distracting you, but they provide no satisfaction. When you get that gnawing sensation around the edges of your soul, return to Me. *Your soul will be satisfied as with the richest of foods.*

"Though the mountains be shaken and the hills be removed, yet my unfailing love for you will not be shaken nor my covenant of peace be removed," says the Lord, who has compassion on you.

ISAIAH 54:10

"Cease striving and know that I am God; I will be exalted among the nations, I will be exalted in the earth."

PSALM 46:10 NASB

O God, you are my God, earnestly I seek you; my soul thirsts for you, my body longs for you, in a dry and weary land where there is no water. I have seen you in the sanctuary and beheld your power and your glory. Because your love is better than life, my lips will glorify you. I will praise you as long as I live, and in your name I will lift up my hands. My soul will be satisfied as with the richest of foods; with singing lips my mouth will praise you.

PSALM 63:1–5

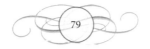

RENEWING YOUR MIND

A HAPPY HEART IS GOOD MEDICINE, AND A CHEERFUL MIND WORKS HEALING. You may think you need to experience healing *first* in order to gain a cheerful heart and mind. However, you have a powerful source of happiness within you: the Holy Spirit! He can empower you to live above your circumstances. When your heart is heavy, ask Him to fill it with buoyant cheerfulness. He takes pleasure in doing this as you entrust yourself into His capable care.

Your heart and mind are intricately connected. It is impossible to have a happy heart when your mind is full of negative thoughts. Left to itself, your mind can become "the devil's workshop"—pulling you away from Me. This is why you need to exert control over your thinking. Ask the Holy Spirit to help you; invite Him to control your mind. Look at your thoughts in His holy Light, and reject those that are unfitting for a child of the King.

I will help you replace lies and partial truths with absolute truth. As I refresh your mind with promises of My constant Love and the eternal home awaiting you, heavenly Light shines powerfully into your heart. Bask in this cheery Light, while My healing Presence permeates you deeply—all the way down to your bones!

*A happy heart is good medicine and a cheerful mind
works healing, but a broken spirit dries up the bones.*

PROVERBS 17:22 AMP

*"And I will pray the Father, and He will give you
another Helper, that He may abide with you forever."*

JOHN 14:16 NKJV

*The mind of sinful man is death, but the mind
controlled by the Spirit is life and peace.*

ROMANS 8:6

*"In My Father's house are many mansions;
if it were not so, I would have told you.
I go to prepare a place for you."*

JOHN 14:2 NKJV

THE FUTURE

I CAN FIT EVERYTHING INTO MY MAJESTIC PLAN FOR GOOD, INCLUDING THE THINGS YOU WISH WERE DIFFERENT. How you long to see that all-embracing pattern—though you wouldn't understand it even if I showed you!

Your current situation feels like a gigantic mistake to you—something you should have been able to prevent. I urge you not to indulge in obsessing about what you could have done differently, for that is an exercise in unreality: The past cannot be different from what has actually occurred. I want to help you make a new beginning instead, starting right where you are.

NOW is the only place to begin anew: It's the unique intersection of time and space you currently inhabit, and it's the space-time location where I intend for you to live. Some things—many things—may be beyond you, but you are capable of living joyfully in the present. After all, you are communicating with Me, your Savior and Lord, this very moment. You can also handle the next moment as it comes—and the next.

What you find most difficult to accept is the way the future looks to you: basing your predictions on current circumstances. But the future is one of those

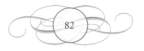

secret things beyond your domain. Release it to Me, the rightful Owner. Refuse to worry about the future, and you will find your resources for today quite sufficient. Remember that I am part of those resources, and *nothing is impossible with Me!*

We are assured and know that [God being a partner in their labor] all things work together and are [fitting into a plan] for good to and for those who love God and are called according to [His] design and purpose.

ROMANS 8:28 AMP

The secret things belong unto the LORD our God, but the things revealed belong to us and to our children forever, that we may follow the words of this law.

DEUTERONOMY 29:29

For nothing is impossible with God.

LUKE 1:37

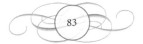

DEPENDING ON HIM

I AM CONSTANTLY CONSCIOUS OF YOUR THOUGHTS. Sometimes your mind creates so many plans that they get tangled up in each other. The longer you indulge in obsessive planning, the farther you roam from awareness of My Presence. Although you may think you are *planning your way*, I am actually the One who *directs your steps*. However, you can choose the hard way (ignoring Me) or the right way (seeking My will). Be thankful for the mental confusion that occurs when you're overly focused on your myriad plans. It can help to simply stop and laugh at yourself at such times. The most important response, though, is to turn back to Me *quickly*—saving precious time and energy.

As you entrust your concerns to Me, I receive them into My care and keeping. This lightens your load and helps you gain traction so you can move forward in dependence on Me. I don't guarantee you a trouble-free journey, but I do promise to make your life meaningful. *I will instruct you and teach you in the way you should go; I will counsel you and watch over you.* Treasure My teaching in your heart, for it is not your plans but *My counsel that will stand.*

The mind of man plans his way,
but the LORD directs his steps.
PROVERBS 16:9 NASB

I know, O LORD, that a man's life is not his own;
it is not for man to direct his steps.
JEREMIAH 10:23

I will instruct you and teach you in the way you
should go; I will counsel you and watch over you.
PSALM 32:8

There are many plans in a man's heart, nevertheless
the LORD's counsel—that will stand.
PROVERBS 19:21 NKJV

EMPTINESS

COME TO ME WITH YOUR ACHING EMPTINESS. Take time with Me so I can fill you with Joy in My Presence. I crafted you as a dependent being, needing many resources outside yourself—air, food, water, shelter, clothing, and so on. Mankind has long recognized these basic needs. However, even when such needs are fully met, there is something vital missing: a living relationship with Me. I am the only One who can satisfy your soul-hunger. Open your heart and soul to Me, and let the joyous abundance of My Presence flow into you.

Since I am *the same yesterday and today and forever*, there could never be a time when you might find Me lacking. It is crucial not only to know this truth but also to believe it wholeheartedly. Whenever you are feeling empty, *come boldly to My throne of grace*. Pour out your heart to Me and allow Me to help you. Confess not only your neediness but also the idolatrous ways you have tried to satisfy your needs. Cooperate with Me as I cleanse your heart of idols. Then, lift up empty hands of faith to receive all that I have for you. Thus you can enjoy many blessings even while living in a deeply fallen world. This is a mere foretaste of the endless pleasures I have reserved for you in paradise.

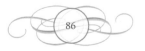

You have made known to me the path of life; you will fill me with joy in your presence, with eternal pleasures at your right hand.

PSALM 16:11

My soul will be satisfied as with the richest of foods; with singing lips my mouth will praise you.

PSALM 63:5

Jesus Christ is the same yesterday and today and forever.

HEBREWS 13:8

Let us therefore come boldly to the throne of grace, that we may obtain mercy and find grace to help in time of need.

HEBREWS 4:16 NKJV

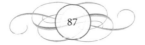

DESIRING HIM

You will seek Me and find Me when you seek Me with all your heart. I know the full extent of your weaknesses, and I realize that seeking Me wholeheartedly requires massive, sustained effort. I understand the brokenness within you and all around you. You are easily distracted by this disjointed world and by your restless thoughts. I don't expect perfection in your pursuit of Me; it's not about that at all. It is the effort itself that pleases Me—seeking Me even though it's so hard.

Actually, the strenuousness of this pursuit blesses you! As you strive to find Me in your moments, your focus is on Me. While you plow your way toward Me through countless distractions, your awareness of Me increases. Even if you don't *feel* close to Me, you find yourself communicating with Me. So there is a sense in which your efforts to find Me are self-fulfilling: I am richly present in your striving. As a result, you feel more alive—more solid and real—when you are actively pursuing Me.

Your willingness to pour yourself into this quest delights My heart. This challenging journey is all about perseverance. As long as you continue seeking Me, you are on the right path. My Presence continually moves along before you—keeping you from stagnating and showing you the way forward. In spite of the difficulties of the arduous trail you are following, your success is certain: *I will be found by you!*

> *"You will seek me and find me when*
> *you seek me with all your heart. I will be*
> *found by you," declares the LORD . . .*
> JEREMIAH 29:13–14

> *Therefore, since we are surrounded by such a great*
> *cloud of witnesses, let us throw off everything that*
> *hinders and the sin that so easily entangles, and let*
> *us run with perseverance the race marked out for us.*
> HEBREWS 12:1

> *And not only that, but we also glory in tribulations,*
> *knowing that tribulation produces perseverance . . .*
> ROMANS 5:3 NKJV

> *For this very reason, make every effort to add to your faith*
> *goodness; and to goodness, knowledge; and to knowledge,*
> *self-control; and to self-control, perseverance; and*
> *to perseverance, godliness . . .*
> 2 PETER 1:5–6

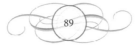

ABIDING IN HIM

I WANT YOU TO LIVE CLOSE TO ME, SEEING THINGS FROM MY PERSPECTIVE MORE AND MORE. *Walk as a child of Light,* for My radiance is all around you and also within you; it transforms you inside and out. Remember that *you were once darkness* until My Spirit quickened you to Life, empowering you to live in My holy Presence. Dwell on this blessed remembrance until gratitude for My *glorious grace* wells up within you.

Trust Me to lead you step by step through each day. I provide sufficient Light for only one day at a time. If you try to look into the future, you will find yourself peering into darkness: *My Face shines upon you* only in the present! This is where you find My gracious Love that never fails you. Live ever so near Me—flourishing in My transforming Light.

*For you were once darkness, but now you are light
in the Lord. Walk as children of light.*
EPHESIANS 5:8 NKJV

*For he chose us in him before the creation of the world
to be holy and blameless in his sight. In love he
predestined us to be adopted as his sons through Jesus
Christ, in accordance with his pleasure and will—
to the praise of his glorious grace, which he
has freely given us in the One he loves.*
EPHESIANS 1:4–6

*The LORD make His face shine upon you,
and be gracious to you.*
NUMBERS 6:25 NKJV

*Planted in the house of the LORD, they will
flourish in the courts of our God.*
PSALM 92:13 NASB

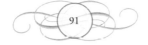

HIS LOVE

MY LOVE FOR YOU IS UNQUENCHABLE. It is even stronger than the bond between a mother and her baby. *Though she may forget the baby at her breast, I will not forget you!* You are so precious to Me that *I have engraved you on the palms of both My hands.* So, forgetting you is out of the question. Not only do I remember you constantly, I also have compassion on you continually.

I want you to *really come to know—practically, through experience—My Love, which far surpasses mere knowledge.* The Holy Spirit, who lives in your inner-most being, will help in this amorous quest. Ask Him to fill you up completely with My fullness so that you may have *the richest measure of the divine Presence:* becoming *a body wholly filled and flooded* with Me! Thus you can experience My Love in full measure.

Many waters cannot quench love, nor can the floods drown it. If a man would give for love all the wealth of his house, it would be utterly despised.
SONG OF SONGS 8:7 NKJV

"Can a mother forget the baby at her breast and have no compassion on the child she has borne? Though she may forget, I will not forget you! See, I have engraved you on the palms of My hands . . ."
ISAIAH 49:15–16

"I will betroth you to me forever; I will betroth you in righteousness and justice, in love and compassion."
HOSEA 2:19

[That you may really come] to know [practically, through experience for yourselves] the love of Christ, which far surpasses mere knowledge [without experience]; that you may be filled [through all your being] unto all the fullness of God [may have the richest measure of the divine Presence, and become a body wholly filled and flooded with God Himself]!
EPHESIANS 3:19 AMP

SORROW

WHEN YOU'RE FEELING SAD, I WANT YOU TO ANTICIPATE FEELING JOYFUL AGAIN. This takes the sting out of your sorrow, because you know it is only temporary. Sadness tends to duplicate itself along the timeline—convincing you that you will always be unhappy. But that is a lie! I urge you to turn away from the lie, choosing rather to trust Me and all I have promised you. The truth is, *all* My children have infinite Joy ahead of them: reserved in heaven, guaranteed throughout eternity! *No one can take this away from you.*

While you are journeying toward heaven, your earthly path has many ups and downs. Though your down times are uncomfortable, they are not worthless. Pain and struggle can be highly productive when you trust Me in the midst of suffering. Your anguish is comparable to a woman enduring labor pains: Her suffering is very real, and she may wonder how much longer she can bear so much pain. However, all this agony produces a wonderful result—a newborn baby. The mother's memories of her suffering retreat to the background of her mind as she focuses on this joyous gift. While you labor through your earthly afflictions, keep your eyes on the promised reward: boundless Joy

in heaven! Even now you can enjoy growing awareness of Me. No matter what is happening, there is *fullness of Joy* to be found in My Presence.

"Therefore you now have sorrow; but I will see you again and your heart will rejoice, and your joy no one will take from you."
JOHN 16:22 NKJV

A woman giving birth to a child has pain because her time has come; but when her baby is born she forgets the anguish because of her joy that a child is born into the world.
JOHN 16:21

You will show me the path of life; in Your presence is fullness of joy; at Your right hand are pleasures forevermore.
PSALM 16:11 NKJV

JOY

WHAT I SEARCH FOR IN MY CHILDREN IS AN AWAKENED SOUL THAT THRILLS TO THE JOY OF MY PRESENCE! However, you are often subject to a slumbering soul: taking for granted your life with all its blessings, being overly focused on negative things, buying into the world's version of the good life. I want to help you break free from these worldly weights so your soul can soar in the heights with Me.

Yearning for an awakened soul is half the battle. Many of My children view devotion to Me as a duty, and they look elsewhere for their pleasures. They fail to understand that the *Joy of My Presence* outshines even the most delightful earthly joy.

Of course, it is not an either/or situation. You don't have to choose between enjoying Me or enjoying the many good gifts I provide. It is simply a matter of priorities: I want you to treasure Me above all else.

The more fully you enjoy Me, the more capacity you have to appreciate the blessings I shower upon you. As you delight in Me, I am free to bless you bountifully. If you keep Me first in your life, My good gifts will not become idols. *Delight yourself in Me, and I will give you the desires and secret petitions of your heart.*

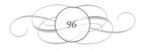

*For the eyes of the LORD range
throughout the earth to strengthen those
whose hearts are fully committed to him.*

2 CHRONICLES 16:9

*You have made known to me the paths of life;
you will fill me with joy in your presence.*

ACTS 2:28

*Every good and perfect gift is from above, coming
down from the Father of the heavenly lights, who
does not change like shifting shadows.*

JAMES 1:17

*Delight yourself also in the Lord, and He will give
you the desires and secret petitions of your heart.*

PSALM 37:4 AMP

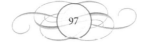

TRUST

TRUST IN ME WITH ALL YOUR HEART AND MIND, AND DO NOT LEAN ON YOUR OWN UNDERSTANDING. *In all your ways acknowledge Me, and I will make your path straight.* Such complete and utter confidence in Me has been your goal for years, but you continue to struggle with this. The main culprit is your mind's ravenous appetite for understanding, fueled by a strong desire to feel in control of your life. You want to trust Me wholeheartedly, but you feel stuck.

Beloved, your desire to rely on Me wholly is a worthy goal. Now also believe that I am providing training through your life experiences, and that many of the difficulties you encounter are designed to help in this endeavor. Allow Me to do this supernatural work in your heart.

The Holy Spirit will help you think trusting thoughts, but He requires your cooperation. Instead of relying on your understanding to help you feel in control, ask My Spirit to control your mind. Then, wait confidently to see results. As you look to Me— trusting Me, talking with Me—I straighten out the path before you.

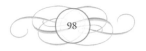

Lean on, trust in, and be confident in the Lord with all your heart and mind and do not rely on your own insight or understanding. In all your ways know, recognize, and acknowledge Him, and He will direct and make straight and plain your paths.

PROVERBS 3:5–6 AMP

Commit your way to the LORD, trust also in Him, and He shall bring it to pass.

PSALM 37:5 NKJV

The mind of sinful man is death, but the mind controlled by the Spirit is life and peace.

ROMANS 8:6

CONDEMNATION

WHENEVER YOUR HEART CONDEMNS YOU, CALL OUT TO ME: "JESUS, HELP ME!" Your heart and mind are battlefields: targets for *the evil one's flaming arrows* of accusation. In order to extinguish those fiery missiles, you must use your *shield of faith* skillfully. When you cry out to Me for help, you demonstrate genuine faith and I join you in the battle. I remind you that I have already paid the full penalty for *all* your sins.

It is crucial to understand that your conscience is imperfect. Many of its accusations are based on lies. You need to listen less to it and more to Me through My Spirit and My Word. You will continue to sin till you leave this world, but I have provided an effective way of dealing with sin—*godly sorrow*. This growth-promoting sorrow is motivated by love and concern for all those whom you have hurt (including Me). It is a work of the Holy Spirit, and it brings real repentance that *leaves no regret*.

When your heart condemns you, remember that *I am greater than your heart and I know all things.* Come confidently and gratefully into My loving Presence.

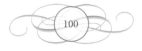

*For if our heart condemns us, God is greater
than our heart, and knows all things.*

1 JOHN 3:20 NKJV

*In addition to all this, take up the shield of faith,
with which you can extinguish all the
flaming arrows of the evil one.*

EPHESIANS 6:16

*Then I heard a loud voice in heaven say: "Now have
come the salvation and the power and the kingdom
of our God, and the authority of his Christ. For the
accuser of our brothers, who accuses them before our
God day and night, has been hurled down."*

REVELATION 12:10

*Godly sorrow brings repentance that leads to salvation
and leaves no regret, but worldly sorrow brings death.*

2 CORINTHIANS 7:10

HOPE

THOUGH DIFFICULTIES ABOUND IN THIS WORLD, REJOICE THAT I AM ALWAYS PRESENT WITH YOU. I can enable you to cope with any and all circumstances, strengthening you as you look trustingly to Me. No matter how hopeless your situation may seem, I assure you that *all things are possible with Me.*

I am the Truth, and therefore I am true to all My promises. They provide a rock-solid foundation on which you can *live and move and have your being.* Since I am the living Word, affirming your trust in My promises is an excellent way to draw near Me. As you bask in the beauty of My Presence, you may find yourself wanting to praise Me. Do not restrain that holy impulse; instead, give it voice. While you are worshiping Me, new hope will grow within you.

Hope in Me, for you will again praise Me for the help of My Presence.

God is our refuge and strength,
an ever-present help in trouble.
PSALM 46:1

Jesus looked at them and said,
"With man this is impossible, but not with God;
all things are possible with God."
MARK 10:27

"In him we live and move and have our being." As some
of your own poets have said, "We are his offspring."
ACTS 17:28

In the beginning was the Word, and the Word
was with God, and the Word was God.
JOHN 1:1

Why are you in despair, O my soul? And why have you
become disturbed within me? Hope in God, for I shall
again praise Him for the help of His presence.
PSALM 42:5 NASB

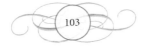

INTIMACY WITH HIM

I AM THE CREATOR OF THE UNIVERSE, YET I CHOOSE TO MAKE MY HUMBLE HOME IN YOUR HEART. It is there you know Me most intimately; it is there I speak to you in holy whispers.

I know this is more than you can fathom—that Someone so great and majestic would choose to live in someone so small and sinful. Your mind almost recoils at the thought of My perfect holiness living in you. It's a thought you do well to struggle with. That shows Me you have some understanding of the absolute purity of My Being. Nonetheless, be assured that your sinfulness cannot taint My holiness. The influence goes the other direction: My righteousness purifies you! Delight in this blessed transaction, gratefully receiving My goodness.

Though you are indeed an exceedingly humble dwelling for Me—the One who also inhabits the highest heavens—I am living in your heart because I deeply desire intimacy with you. You are weak: easily distracted by the noise of the world. Yet I want to help you hear My *gentle whispers* in your heart. You need stillness—outer and inner. Find a quiet place, where the noise of the world is minimal. Then focus your mind on this loving command: *"Cease striving and know that I am God."* Be still, let go, and relax in My Presence while I commune with you in holy whispers.

But in these last days he has spoken to us by his Son, whom he appointed heir of all things, and through whom he made the universe.

HEBREWS 1:2

I pray that out of his glorious riches he may strengthen you with power through his Spirit in your inner being, so that Christ may dwell in your hearts through faith.

EPHESIANS 3:16–17

After the earthquake came a fire, but the LORD was not in the fire. And after the fire came a gentle whisper.

1 KINGS 19:12

"Cease striving and know that I am God;
I will be exalted among the nations,
I will be exalted in the earth."

PSALM 46:10 NASB

HEAVEN

YOUR PRAYERS ARE NOT CRIES IN THE DARK. On the contrary, they rise to My kingdom of eternal Light. *Call to Me, and I will answer you, and show you great and mighty things.* Mankind has long been plagued with eyes that do not see what is most important. Many people fail to see the most obvious things: I can perform miracles before their very eyes, yet they see only mundane occurrences or—at best—coincidences. Only *the eyes of your heart* can see spiritual realities.

One of the things I search for among My children is a *teachable* attitude. When you come to Me desirous of learning wondrous *things which you do not know*, I rejoice. A good teacher takes pleasure in a student who really wants to learn, who puts forth extra effort to discover as much as possible. I am the Teacher of teachers, and I delight in your desire to learn amazing, unsearchable things from Me. Your openness to My teaching has a wonderful result: I help you understand at heart level *the hope to which I have called you, the riches of My glorious inheritance* in which you share. You can look forward to living rapturously with Me in the Holy City, where *the Glory of God provides Light.*

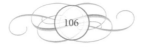

"Call to Me, and I will answer you, and show you great
and mighty things, which you do not know."
JEREMIAH 33:3 NKJV

I pray also that the eyes of your heart may be
enlightened in order that you may know the hope
to which he has called you, the riches of his glorious
inheritance in the saints.
EPHESIANS 1:18

Teach me to do your will, for you are my God;
may your good Spirit lead me on level ground.
PSALM 143:10

The city does not need the sun or the moon
to shine on it, for the glory of God gives it light,
and the Lamb is its lamp.
REVELATION 21:23

CONTROL

ENTRUST YOUR LOVED ONES TO ME. They are much safer with Me than in your clinging hands.

Sometimes you confuse loving others with rescuing them. When a loved one has a problem, you often feel responsible to come up with a solution. Then you plunge headlong into problem-solving mode, as if you're obligated to provide sound advice. I want to help you stop feeling responsible to fix people since that is My role—not yours.

It is My prerogative to bring about change in people's lives as I choose. You can be part of the process, but remember that I am the Author and Director of the drama. You need to follow My script rather than creating your own. Do not usurp My role in people's lives, no matter how much you long to help them.

When you feel compelled to rescue a loved one, take a good look at the quality of your love. Learn from Me, because I have *all authority in heaven and on earth:* I could rescue or control anyone at will. Yet I intentionally created people with the capacity to choose good or evil. I wanted them to be free to love Me—or not. Love that has no choice is not real!

Prayerfully release your loved ones into My protective care. Restrain your urges to solve their problems. Instead, use your time and energy to listen to them and pray for them. Trust in My Love and My infinite wisdom. I can work changes in your loved ones' lives *beyond anything you might ask or imagine.* As you release these precious ones to Me, linger awhile in *My unfailing Love*—for them and also for you.

Then Jesus came to them and said, "All authority in heaven and on earth has been given to me."
MATTHEW 28:18

Now to him who is able to do immeasurably more than all we ask or imagine, according to his power that is at work within us, to him be glory in the church and in Christ Jesus throughout all generations, for ever and ever! Amen.
EPHESIANS 3:20–21

Let the morning bring me word of your unfailing love, for I have put my trust in you. Show me the way I should go, for to you I lift up my soul.
PSALM 143:8

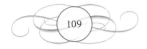

ADVERSITY

WHEN YOU PASS THROUGH THE WATERS, I WILL BE WITH YOU. I want you to trust in My protective Presence even while deep waters of affliction are rising around you. Remember that *you are precious in My sight and I love you*. I will never, ever abandon you! Though you may lose sight of Me, I am constantly aware of you and your circumstances. When you cry out to Me for help, I am already fully apprised of your situation. So you don't need to take time telling Me what is happening or what you think I should do. In the midst of emergencies, short pithy prayers are extremely effective: "Help me, Jesus!" "Show me Your way." *"Your will be done."*

Do not be overly concerned about your feelings during emergencies. The most important thing is that you turn to Me, trusting that I am indeed with you. When you cannot sense My Presence, it is enough to *know* that I love you with compassionate, unfailing Love. If your heart is sinking under waves of panic, don't focus on those feelings. Instead, look up to Me! As *your soul clings to Me, My right hand will uphold you*—keeping you safe in turbulent waters.

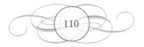

"When you pass through the waters,
I will be with you; and through the rivers,
they will not overflow you. . . . Since you are
precious in My sight . . . and I love you . . ."
ISAIAH 43:2–4 NASB

Your kingdom come. Your will be done
on earth as it is in heaven.
MATTHEW 6:10 NKJV

Though he brings grief, he will show compassion,
so great is his unfailing love.
LAMENTATIONS 3:32

My soul clings to you; your right hand upholds me.
PSALM 63:8

TRANSFORMATION

AS THE HOLY SPIRIT CONTROLS YOUR MIND AND ACTIONS MORE FULLY, YOU BECOME FREE IN ME. You are increasingly released to become the one I created you to be.

Freedom through surrender sounds like a contradiction, doesn't it? Yet when My Spirit is controlling your thinking and behavior, you feel more alive, more real, more content! I encourage you to pray, "Holy Spirit, think through me, live through me, love through me." This is a prayer of surrender. Nonetheless, even though you may pray this way, your desire to be in control can sabotage you.

In My kingdom freedom comes from yielding to *My perfect will.* Because I am infinite and you are not, My will may appear to be anything but perfect. Still, I want you to trust Me, even when you cannot understand what I'm doing. The Holy Spirit will help you in this as you invite Him to control your thinking. He lives in the depths of your spirit and knows you better than you know yourself. His work in you can liberate you to become more completely the one I designed you to be.

I am pleased when you ask My Spirit to live and love through you. This is the collaborative way of living

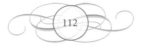

I had in mind when I created mankind. The more you collaborate with Him, the freer you become: free to live exuberantly, to love extravagantly, to know Me in ever-increasing intimacy!

> The mind of sinful man is death, but the mind
> controlled by the Spirit is life and peace.
>
> ROMANS 8:6

> Do not conform any longer to the pattern of this world,
> but be transformed by the renewing of your mind. Then
> you will be able to test and approve what God's will
> is—his good, pleasing and perfect will.
>
> ROMANS 12:2

> In the same way, the Spirit helps us in our weakness.
> We do not know what we ought to pray for, but the Spirit
> himself intercedes for us with groans that words cannot
> express. And he who searches our hearts knows the
> mind of the Spirit, because the Spirit intercedes for
> the saints in accordance with God's will.
>
> ROMANS 8:26–27

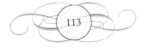

HIS LOVE

FIND COMFORT IN KNOWING I AM PERFECTLY
GOOD AND INFINITELY STRONG. If I were good
but lacking in strength, you would have no *stronghold
in times of trouble*. If I were strong but not totally good,
My massive strength could be terrifying. In fact, My
Power *is* threatening to those who oppose Me. However,
*I am the Good Shepherd; I know My sheep, and My sheep
know Me*. Sheep have nothing to fear from a shepherd
who is good. On the contrary, they feel safe in his protective presence. So it is with Me: You can feel safe and
secure in My sheltering Presence.

The best way to avail yourself of My protection is to trust Me wholeheartedly. *My unfailing Love
surrounds all those who trust in Me*. So your most
important task as a sheep in My pasture is to keep on
trusting Me—the perfect Shepherd of your soul. *Find
rest in Me alone*, for I am a surrounding stronghold of
unfailing Love.

The LORD is good, A stronghold in the day
of trouble; And He knows those who trust in Him.

NAHUM 1:7 NKJV

I am the good shepherd; I know my sheep
and my sheep know me.

JOHN 10:14

Many are the woes of the wicked,
but the LORD's unfailing love surrounds
the man who trusts in him.

PSALM 32:10

My soul finds rest in God alone; my salvation comes
from him. He alone is my rock and my salvation;
he is my fortress, I will never be shaken.

PSALM 62:1–2

PEACE

MY PEACE IS SUCH AN ALL-ENCOMPASSING GIFT THAT IT IS INDEPENDENT OF CIRCUM- STANCES. Though you lose everything else, if you gain My Peace you are rich indeed.

Let that be a deep comfort to you, especially amid the many aspects of your life over which you have no control! When you are feeling at the mercy of your circumstances, My all-encompassing Peace is exactly what you need, even though you sometimes feel unable to receive it. Perhaps that is because you cling to other things—your loved ones, your possessions, your repu- tation. It's as if you are wrapping your fingers tightly around a small copper coin while I am offering you unlimited supplies of pure gold. My desire is to help you treasure My Peace above everything in the world— recognizing it as a supernatural gift, bequeathed to My followers shortly before My death.

A man who knows he will soon die wants to leave something precious with those he loves. Therefore, I "willed" My Peace to My disciples and all who would follow Me. I knew this was a difficult gift to accept, especially in the midst of adversity. So, after My resur- rection, the first words I spoke to My disciples were

"Peace be with you!" They needed this reassurance to reinforce what I taught them before I died. You also need to be reminded of the divine nature of this gift, for *it is not the world's peace I give you:* It is *Peace that transcends all understanding!*

Peace I leave with you; my peace I give you. I do not give to you as the world gives. Do not let your hearts be troubled and do not be afraid.
JOHN 14:27

On the evening of that first day of the week, when the disciples were together, with the doors locked for fear of the Jews, Jesus came and stood among them and said, "Peace be with you!"
JOHN 20:19

Do not be anxious about anything, but in everything, by prayer and petition, with thanksgiving, present your requests to God. And the peace of God, which transcends all understanding, will guard your hearts and our minds in Christ Jesus.
PHILIPPIANS 4:6–7

117

DEPENDING ON HIM

MY POWER FLOWS MOST FREELY INTO WEAK ONES AWARE OF THEIR NEED FOR ME. So take heart: Though the journey you're on is one of faltering steps, such steps of dependence are links to My Presence.

Today you feel the journey more than usual. It's a challenge just to take the next step. Sometimes you get discouraged about your ongoing weaknesses. You know that dependence on Me brings spiritual blessings, yet at times you feel trapped by your limitations. Only the knowledge that I am with you keeps you out of the pit of despair.

Awareness of your need for Me is what creates a strong connection to My Presence. My Power flows into you continually: It gives you strength to take the next step, strength to resist discouragement and despair, strength to know Me in intimate dependence. Only My Power can enable you to live abundantly in the midst of your limitations. Your day-to-day perseverance, in dependence on Me, is every bit as supernatural as an outright miracle. So don't think that your difficulties signify lack of faith or lack of blessing. They are means to help you stay on the path I have chosen for you.

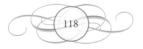

Though the way before you may be steep and rocky, it is nonetheless the path of Life. It is where you encounter My luminous Presence—radiating *Peace that transcends all understanding.*

Though the fig tree does not bud and there are no grapes on the vines, though the olive crop fails and the fields produce no food, though there are no sheep in the pen and no cattle in the stalls, yet I will rejoice in the Lord, I will be joyful in God my Savior. The Sovereign Lord is my strength; he makes my feet like the feet of a deer, he enables me to go on the heights.
HABAKKUK 3:17–19

To him who is able to keep you from falling and to present you before his glorious presence without fault and with great joy—to the only God our Savior be glory, majesty, power and authority, through Jesus Christ our Lord, before all ages, now and forevermore! Amen.
JUDE 1:24–25

And the peace of God, which transcends all understanding, will guard your hearts and your minds in Christ Jesus.
PHILIPPIANS 4:7

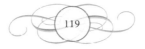

THANKFULNESS

WHENEVER YOU ARE TEMPTED TO GRUMBLE, COME TO ME AND TALK IT OUT. As you open up to Me, I will put My thoughts in your mind and My song in your heart.

There are so many things you would like to be different: in yourself, in others, in the world. Your natural tendency is to brood over these matters rather than to talk them over with Me. The longer you focus on these negatives, the more likely you are to become disgruntled. Even when you control what you say out loud, your thoughts tend to be full of complaints. Let Me help you think My thoughts.

Trust Me by opening up to Me consistently. Don't wait till you're already discouraged to bring Me your concerns. As we talk about these matters, remember to thank Me. In spite of how you're feeling, you can thank Me for listening and caring; also, for loving you enough to die for you. Your gratitude will provide a helpful framework for the things that concern you. As we talk about these things, let *the Light of My Face shine upon you*. Eventually, this heavenly Light will break through the fog in your mind, enabling you to see things from My perspective.

Your communion with Me will bless you in another way also: You will find in My Presence irrepressible Joy. Whether or not I change your circumstances, you will discover I have given you *a new song—a hymn of praise.*

Thanks be to God for his indescribable gift!
2 CORINTHIANS 9:15

The LORD make his face shine upon you
and be gracious to you.
NUMBERS 6:25

You have made known to me the paths of life; you will
fill me with joy in your presence.
ACTS 2:28

He put a new song in my mouth,
a hymn of praise to our God. Many will see
and fear and put their trust in the LORD.
PSALM 40:3

WORRY

Do NOT WORRY ABOUT TOMORROW. This is simple, straightforward teaching, but My followers rarely make it through even one day without breaking this command. It's good that you recognize your inability to live according to this instruction. Your ongoing struggle protects you from self-righteous striving: trying to be good enough to deserve My Love. Nonetheless, I do want to help you with your tendency to worry.

Because your mind is in a fallen condition, it *will* sometimes wander across the timeline into tomorrow's trouble. However, early intervention can minimize the damage. As soon as you realize you're worrying about tomorrow, take action: Simply leave those thoughts where they are (in the unreality of the future), and come quickly back to the present. Since the future has such a strong pull on your mind, it's helpful to direct your thoughts to something that appeals to you in the present—an interesting activity, beautiful weather, a dear friend or family member. At times when nothing about the present day seems appealing, My Presence lovingly awaits your attention. I am always near, so turning your thoughts to Me is an excellent option at *all* times. Come into My joyous Presence, and I will delight you with unmerited Love.

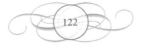

Therefore do not worry about tomorrow,
for tomorrow will worry about itself. Each day
has enough trouble of its own.

MATTHEW 6:34

But because of his great love for us, God,
who is rich in mercy, made us alive with Christ even
when we were dead in transgressions—it is
by grace you have been saved.

EPHESIANS 2:4–5

Therefore, holy brothers, who share in the heavenly
calling, fix your thoughts on Jesus, the apostle and
high priest whom we confess.

HEBREWS 3:1

Then will I go to the altar of God, to God,
my joy and my delight. I will praise you with
the harp, O God, my God.

PSALM 43:4

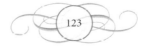

BROKENNESS

NOTHING IS WASTED WHEN IT IS SHARED WITH ME. I can bring *beauty out of the ashes* of lost dreams; I can glean Joy out of sorrow, Peace out of adversity. This divine alchemy will become a reality in your experience as you learn how to share more and more of your life with Me. You believe I *am* capable of creating wholeness out of your brokenness and struggles. So I urge you to bring all these things to Me for transformation, trusting in My healing Presence.

I take great delight in transforming My precious children. Give Me your broken dreams! Release them into My care and keeping. I will not only heal the brokenness, I will give you a new dream—one that is in harmony with My plans for you. As you seek to nurture this budding dream, you will find yourself becoming more content and increasingly aware of My beautiful Presence.

Give Me your sadness and your problems as well. Sorrow shared with Me is permeated with brilliant glitters of Joy—like numerous Christmas lights sparkling in the darkness. Accept adversity as My gift to you. You will find golden pockets of Peace hidden in the hardness of your problems.

I am your devoted Friend and also your King of kings, accomplishing My divine transformation in you. *All things are possible with Me!*

He has sent me to bind up the brokenhearted . . .
and provide for those who grieve in Zion—to bestow
on them a crown of beauty instead of ashes, the oil
of gladness instead of mourning, and a garment
of praise instead of a spirit of despair. They
will be called oaks of righteousness, a planting
of the LORD for the display of his splendor.
ISAIAH 61:1–3

Peace I leave with you; my peace I give to you. I do
not give to you as the world gives. Do not let your
hearts be troubled and do not be afraid.
JOHN 14:27

Jesus looked at them and said, "With man this is
impossible, but with God all things are possible."
MATTHEW 19:26

TRANSFORMATION

SINCE YOU JOINED MY ROYAL FAMILY, I HAVE BROUGHT MUCH LIGHT INTO YOUR LIFE. However, this is only *like the first gleam of dawn* compared with *the full Light of day* that awaits all who walk on *the path of the righteous.* You need My help each moment to keep your feet on this path, and My assistance is available to you every nanosecond of your life. There is no righteousness apart from Me, but I have already secured this glorious gift for you through My completed work on the cross.

I am *the Sun of righteousness,* and there is *healing in My wings.* As you bask in the security of *My* righteousness, My healing Presence transforms you more and more into the treasure I designed you to be.

The full Light of day is glorious beyond description. That Light is blindingly brilliant: too bright for earth's inhabitants. However, when you reach your heavenly home, you will *awake in My likeness.* Your new, imperishable eyes will be able to perceive the full Light of My Glory! *In righteousness you will see My Face*—and *be satisfied.*

The path of the righteous is like the first gleam of dawn,
shining ever brighter till the full light of day.
PROVERBS 4:18

But for you who revere my name,
the sun of righteousness will rise with healing
in its wings. And you will go out and leap
like calves released from the stall.
MALACHI 4:2

Saul got up from the ground, but when he opened his
eyes he could see nothing. So they led him by the
hand into Damascus. For three days he was blind,
and did not eat or drink anything.
ACTS 9:8–9

As for me, I will see Your face in righteousness;
I shall be satisfied when I awake in Your likeness.
PSALM 17:15 NKJV

RENEWING YOUR MIND

Do not be conformed to this world, but be transformed by the renewing of your mind. I understand your struggles; I know that the world exerts relentless pressure on you, trying to squeeze you into its mold. This is why you need time alone with Me. When you open up to Me and invite Me to transform you, I can work freely in you and accomplish amazing things. One of My most challenging tasks is renovating your mind, and My Spirit is always at work on this project. He does not overwhelm you with His Power. Instead, He prompts you gently and convicts you cleanly—showing you where you need to make changes and helping you develop new attitudes.

Many Christians are unable to discern My will because their minds are entangled in worldliness. The glitter and glamour of this world distract them from Me, so they do not sense My nearness. As you are transformed by the renewing of your mind, you progress in your ability to discern My good and perfect will. You also become increasingly aware of My loving Presence with you. This awareness is so pleasurable that it draws you ever closer to Me—increasing the effectiveness of My work in you, creating an upward spiral of transformation. Thus you grow not only closer to Me but also more like Me. This is a foretaste of what is to come when I am fully revealed: *You will be like Me, for you will see Me as I am.*

And do not be conformed to this world,
but be transformed by the renewing of your mind,
that you may prove what is that good and
acceptable and perfect will of God.
ROMANS 12:2 NKJV

Now the Lord is the Spirit, and where the Spirit
of the Lord is, there is freedom.
2 CORINTHIANS 3:17

Beloved, now we are children of God;
and it has not yet been revealed what we shall be,
but we know that when He is revealed, we shall
be like Him, for we shall see Him as He is.
1 JOHN 3:2 NKJV

RESTING IN HIM

MY PRESENCE WILL GO WITH YOU, AND I WILL GIVE YOU REST. Sometimes when you are quite weary, all you can think about is finding rest. As a result, your awareness of My Presence grows dim. I assure you, though, that even when your attention falters, Mine remains steadfast. Rejoice that the One who always takes care of you has an infinite attention span!

Even the most devoted parents cannot be constantly attentive to their children: They have to sleep *some* of the time. Also, they can be distracted by other demands on their attention. Many deeply loved children have drowned when their devoted parents took their eyes off them ever so briefly. Only I have the capability of watching over My beloved children continually— without the least interruption.

Instead of worrying about where and when you will find rest, remember that I have promised to provide it for you. Worrying wastes vast quantities of energy—the very thing you need most to help you reach a resting place. If you were driving a car with little gas in the tank and the nearest service station was far away, you would drive carefully and steadily— so as to minimize gas consumption. Similarly, when you are low on energy you need to minimize consumption of *this* precious commodity. Go gently and steadily through your day, looking to Me for help. Rest in the knowledge that My watch-care over you is perfect. Thus, you make the most of your limited energy. Whenever you are struggling with weariness, *come to Me and I will give you rest.*

And He said, "My Presence will go with you,
and I will give you rest."
EXODUS 33:14 NKJV

My help comes from the LORD, the Maker of heaven
and earth. He will not let your foot slip—he who
watches over you will not slumber.
PSALM 121:2–3

"Come to me, all you who are weary and
burdened, and I will give you rest."
MATTHEW 11:28

TRUST

LAY YOUR REQUESTS BEFORE ME AND WAIT IN EXPECTATION. Waiting and trusting are ever so closely connected. The more you trust Me, the more you can wait with a positive attitude. Meeting with Me each morning is a profound demonstration of trust. This practice helps you begin the day with a thankful heart—receiving it as a precious gift from Me.

Waiting in My Presence has beneficial "side effects," so don't be overly focused on getting the answers you seek. In My holy Light you relate to Me as creature to Creator, as clay to Potter. This humbles you and helps you worship Me as I truly am. Many people create in their minds a convenient god who suits their goals and lifestyle. They may call this god by My Name, but they are actually practicing idolatry. You need to search the Scriptures to protect yourself from this tragic deception. As you read My Word, ask the Holy Spirit to illumine your mind so you can see Me more clearly—without distortions.

Feel free to bring Me many requests, because your world is brimming with neediness—as are you. While you watch and wait in My Presence, look trustingly up to Me. I speak graciously to your heart, assuring you of *My unfailing Love.*

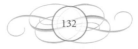

132

In the morning, O Lord, You hear my voice;
in the morning I lay my requests before
You and wait in expectation.

PSALM 5:3

Yet, O Lord, you are our Father. We are the clay,
you are the potter; we are all the work of your hand.

ISAIAH 64:8

But the hour is coming, and now is, when the true
worshipers will worship the Father in spirit and truth;
for the Father is seeking such to worship Him.

JOHN 4:23 NKJV

But I trust in your unfailing love; my heart
rejoices in your salvation.

PSALM 13:5

INTIMACY WITH HIM

YOUR SOUL CAN GRASP MATTERS THAT ARE
TOO DEEP FOR YOUR MIND'S UNDERSTANDING.
One of these deep truths is My Father's perfect Love
for you—*the very Love He has for Me*. I came to live
on your planet so I could make this indescribable Love
real to you.

Anyone who has seen Me has seen the Father. Therefore, as you get to know Me better, you simultaneously
come to know the Father more fully. The better you
know Us, the more Our sacred Love dwells in you.

My Love and My Presence are inseparable: *I Myself*
live in you! Thus, there are no limits to the depth of
intimacy you and I can experience. I know everything
about you—including your deepest desires and darkest
secrets. I understand perfectly things about you which
you have yet to discover. However, My knowledge of you
is not clinical or detached: I view you through the eyes
of a passionate Lover! I invite you to open your heart
and soul fully to Me; this will increase our intimacy,
enabling you to experience more of My boundless Love.
For now you *know in part (imperfectly)*, but in heaven
you will *know and understand fully—even as you have
been fully, clearly known.*

I have made you known to them, and will continue to make you known in order that the love you have for me may be in them and that I myself may be in them.

JOHN 17:26

Jesus answered: "Don't you know me, Philip, even after I have been among you such a long time? Anyone who has seen me has seen the Father. How can you say, 'Show us the Father'?"

JOHN 14:9

Deep calls to deep in the roar of your waterfalls; all your waves and breakers have swept over me.

PSALM 42:7

For now we are looking in a mirror that gives only a dim (blurred) reflection [of reality as in a riddle or enigma], but then [when perfection comes] we shall see in reality and face to face! Now I know in part (imperfectly), but then I shall know and understand fully and clearly, even in the same manner as I have been fully and clearly known and understood [by God].

1 CORINTHIANS 13:12 AMP

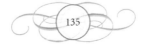

WEAKNESS

I AM ABLE TO SYMPATHIZE WITH YOUR WEAK-
NESSES, FOR I HAVE BEEN TEMPTED IN EVERY
WAY. Not only do I understand you perfectly with all
your weakness, but I have infinite resources because I
am both Man and God. When friends try to help you
with your problems, their own flaws and sinfulness can
get in the way. I, on the other hand, comprehend you
from both a divine, all-knowing perspective and a sin-
less human viewpoint. During my thirty-three years on
earth I experienced terrible temptations, and I had to
endure everything *without sinning*—in order to be your
Savior. If you ever doubt My Love for you, just look at
all I suffered so that I could spend eternity with you! *Amen*

When you are going through painful trials, it is
tempting to blame Me because you know I have unlimited Power to intervene. However, I refrained from
using that Power to save Myself from brutal torture and
execution. Whenever I allow you to suffer, try to see it
as My vote of confidence in you. It's a way of affirming
you as a member of My royal family: *a co-heir with Me.*
Call upon Me when you are in the midst of trials, and I
will be ever so near you—entering into your suffering.
Remember that I allow you to *share in My sufferings in
order that you may also share in My Glory.*

*For we do not have a high priest who is
unable to sympathize with our weaknesses, but we
have one who has been tempted in every way,
just as we are—yet was without sin.*

HEBREWS 4:15

*For consider Him who endured such hostility from
sinners against Himself, lest you become weary
and discouraged in your souls.*

HEBREWS 12:3 NKJV

*Now if we are children, then we are heirs—heirs of
God and co-heirs with Christ, if indeed we share in his
sufferings in order that we may also share in his glory.*

ROMANS 8:17

PRAYER

MARVEL AT THE WONDER OF BEING ABLE TO COMMUNE WITH THE KING OF THE UNIVERSE ANY TIME. Please don't take this awesome prayer-privilege for granted! Don't let foolish arrogance step in either, making you act as if you're doing Me a favor by spending time talking with Me.

The best antidote to such foolishness is recognizing it and repenting of it. Then remember who I Am: *King of kings and Lord of lords, dwelling in dazzlingly unapproachable Light.* My eyes are like *blazing fire.* My voice is like *the sound of rushing waters.* My face is like *the sun shining in all its brilliance.* Yet I am also your Shepherd, tenderly leading you step by step through your life. I want you to realize how precious you are to Me—how much I delight in you. I long for you to reciprocate by delighting in Me.

I listen to your heart as well as to your words. When you approach My *throne of grace* joyfully, anticipating the wondrous pleasure of communing with Me, both you and I are blessed!

God, the blessed and only Ruler, the King of kings and Lord of lords, who alone is immortal and who lives in unapproachable light, whom no one has seen or can see. To him be honor and might forever. Amen.

1 TIMOTHY 6:15–16

His head and hair were white like wool, as white as snow, and his eyes were like blazing fire. His feet were like bronze glowing in a furnace, and his voice was like the sound of rushing waters. In his right hand he held seven stars, and out of his mouth came a sharp double-edged sword. His face was like the sun shining in all its brilliance.

REVELATION 1:14–16

Delight yourself in the LORD and he will give you the desires of your heart.

PSALM 37:4

Let us then approach the throne of grace with confidence, so that we may receive mercy and find grace to help us in our time of need.

HEBREWS 4:16

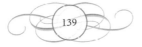

FEAR

FEAR OF MAN WILL PROVE TO BE A SNARE, BUT
WHOEVER TRUSTS IN ME IS KEPT SAFE. You're
beginning to realize how much your life is hampered
by fear of man. This condition has been so much a part
of your daily existence, that you failed to recognize it
until recently. Now that you realize what's going on, let
Me help you break free from this fear of other people's
disapproval.

I will give you a two-pronged approach for dealing with this crippling condition. First, replace your
fear of displeasing people with eagerness to please
Me—the Lord of the universe. Make *pleasing Me* your
highest priority. Include Me in your thinking whenever you are making plans or decisions. Let your desire
to enjoy My approval shine brightly, illuminating your
thoughts and choices.

The second way to free yourself from fear of man
is to develop deeper trust in Me. Instead of trying to
please people so they will give you what you want,
trust in Me—the Supplier of *all your needs*. My glorious riches never run short, nor does My Love for you.
People can easily deceive you, promising you things
with no intention of following through. Even if they

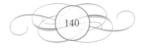

140

mean well at the time, they may change their minds later on. Because *I remain the same forever*, I am absolutely dependable. Trusting in people is risky. Trusting in Me is wise: It keeps you safe.

*Fear of man will prove to be a snare, but whoever
trusts in the Lord is kept safe.*
PROVERBS 29:25

*So we make it our goal to please him, whether we are at
home in the body or away from it.*
2 CORINTHIANS 5:9

*And my God will meet all your needs according
to his glorious riches in Christ Jesus.*
PHILIPPIANS 4:19

*But you remain the same,
and your years will never end.*
PSALM 102:27

GRACE

Even your mistakes can be recycled into something good through My transforming grace. Do you believe this—believe that your mistakes can be used for good in My kingdom?

When you know you've made mistakes, it's easy to start fantasizing about *what might have been*—if only you had acted or chosen differently. But this accomplishes nothing!

The best strategy for accepting yourself when you've made mistakes is to draw near Me. This nearness helps you see things from My perspective. You tend to view yourself as someone who should be almost perfect, making very few errors. My perspective is quite different: I see you as My beloved child—weak in many ways, prone to wandering from Me. However, your weakness and waywardness cannot diminish My constant Love for you. Moreover, My infinite wisdom enables Me to take your errors and weave them into an intricate work that is good.

You need to accept not only yourself but also the choices you have made. Fantasizing about having done things differently is a time-wasting trap. The more you fantasize, the further from Me you wander. When you

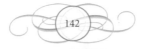

realize this has happened, turn around and run back to Me! Take time to talk with Me and relax in My Presence. Your perfectionist tendencies will dissolve as you soak in My transforming grace.

As a father has compassion on his children, so the LORD has compassion on those who fear him; for he knows how we are formed, he remembers that we are dust.
PSALM 103:13–14

May your unfailing love be my comfort, according to your promise to your servant.
PSALM 119:76

In him we have redemption through his blood, the forgiveness of sins, in accordance with the riches of God's grace that he lavished on us with all wisdom and understanding.
EPHESIANS 1:7–8

FREEDOM IN HIM

I HAVE SAVED YOU TO THE UTTERMOST— PERFECTLY, TOTALLY, FOR ALL ETERNITY! So your salvation is absolutely assured. I want you to live in the freedom that flows from this indescribable gift. That is why I came into the world: to *set you free* from sin and bondage. Let the glorious truth of the gospel soak into your innermost being, and you will grow increasingly free.

I am the ideal Intercessor for you, because I understand you completely. I lived as a Man in your world for thirty-three years, and I know firsthand how hard it is to resist temptation. *I was led by the Spirit into the desert to be tempted by the devil* for forty days and nights, with nothing to eat. Throughout my life on earth I endured one temptation after the other. When I was being crucified, people taunted Me mercilessly— saying they would believe in Me if I *came down from the cross*. I was fully capable of performing this miracle, which made the temptation all the more agonizing.

Now *I live to make intercession for you*. Since I am infinite in all My ways, I am never too busy: I am always available to help you. When you languish in the shadows, feeling bad about yourself, I wait for you. When

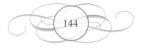

you come freely into My bright Presence, seeking My help, I joyfully respond to your needs. Remember that I am the One who understands you perfectly and loves you eternally.

Therefore He is also able to save to the uttermost those who come to God through Him, since He always lives to make intercession for them.
HEBREWS 7:25 NKJV

Then you will know the truth, and the truth will set you free.
JOHN 8:32

Then Jesus was led by the Spirit into the desert to be tempted by the devil. After fasting forty days and forty nights, he was hungry.
MATTHEW 4:1–2

"Let this Christ, this King of Israel, come down now from the cross, that we may see and believe." Those crucified with him also heaped insults on him.
MARK 15:32

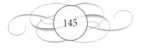

ATTITUDE

IF IT IS POSSIBLE, AS FAR AS IT DEPENDS ON YOU, LIVE AT PEACE WITH EVERYONE. Most people prefer to live peacefully with others, but when there are conflicts, many wait for the other person to make the first move. Problems inevitably arise when *both* parties wait for the other to take the first step. That's why the apostle Paul instructs each offended person to move toward the other. If even one of the two follows this teaching, there is hope for restoring the relationship.

Paul's teaching reflects My own: Reconciling with an offended brother or sister should be done before *offering your gift at the altar*. In other words, restoring peace in your relationships—*as far as it depends on you*—is a prerequisite for participating in worship. Paul's command includes an important qualifying phrase: *if it is possible*. You might do all the right things without achieving reconciliation. In that case, you are free—to live and love and worship with a clear conscience.

To *live at peace with everyone*, you need to control not only what you say and do but also what you think. It's common to assume that your thoughts about others don't matter much, as long as you keep them to yourself.

However, I am fully aware of all your thoughts. When you indulge in negative thinking about someone, your relationship with that person is damaged. Those hurtful thoughts also affect your relationship with Me, and they may have a depressive effect on you. The remedy lies in turning to Me and seeking My forgiveness. Then, ask My Spirit to control your mind and help you think *My* thoughts. This is the way of *Life and Peace*.

*If it is possible, as far as it depends on you,
live at peace with everyone.*
ROMANS 12:18

*Therefore, if you are offering your gift at the
altar and there remember that your brother has
something against you, leave your gift there in front
of the altar. First go and be reconciled to your
brother; then come and offer your gift.*
MATTHEW 5:23–24

*The mind of sinful man is death, but the mind
controlled by the Spirit is life and peace.*
ROMANS 8:6

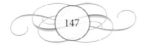

HIS SUFFICIENCY

I AM TEACHING YOU THE SECRET OF BEING CONTENT IN ANY AND EVERY SITUATION. This secret is all about *Me*—who I am and what I offer you. I am your Creator and King, your Savior and Shepherd. I offer you Myself in all My Power and Glory. I am the only One who can empower you to find contentment in all circumstances.

I have promised to *supply all your need according to My riches in Glory*. The greater your need, the more I invite you into the mysterious depths of My Being. Intimacy with Me *gives you strength*; it also fills you with transcendent Joy.

Some of My followers are comfortable with being in need but struggle with having plenty. When I supply abundantly, they feel unworthy—even guilty. How this grieves Me! Imagine a wealthy parent giving a desired, expensive gift to his beloved child. The expected response would be pleasure and gratitude. If instead the child felt unworthy of this extravagant gift, the generous parent would feel deeply disappointed and hurt. That is how I feel when My children balk at receiving abundance from Me. The secret of being content is childlike trust in Me: My infinite riches and generous

Love. Do not expect to understand My ways with you. Remember that *My ways and thoughts are higher than yours—as the heavens are higher than the earth.*

I know what it is to be in need, and I know what it is to have plenty. I have learned the secret of being content in any and every situation, whether well fed or hungry, whether living in plenty or in want. I can do everything through him who gives me strength.

PHILIPPIANS 4:12–13

And my God shall supply all your need according to His riches in glory by Christ Jesus.

PHILIPPIANS 4:19 NKJV

"For My thoughts are not your thoughts, nor are your ways My ways," says the Lord. "For as the heavens are higher than the earth, so are My ways higher than your ways, and My thoughts than your thoughts."

ISAIAH 55:8–9 NKJV

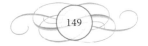

149

DEPENDING ON HIM

I HAVE CALLED YOU OUT OF DARKNESS INTO MY MARVELOUS LIGHT. I brought you not only *out of darkness* but also *into* My royal family. I clothed you with My own *robe of righteousness*—making you fit for My kingdom. You are one of *My own special people:* You belong to Me, and I delight in you.

I have chosen to use imperfect ones like you to *proclaim My praises*. I know you cannot do this as well as you would like. The truth is, without My help you can't do it at all. This gap between My call on your life and your ability to respond is part of My plan. It heightens your awareness of your utter insufficiency. Because you are Mine, I allow you to connect your deep inadequacy to My boundless sufficiency. Instead of focusing on your imperfection, make every effort to stay connected with Me. The more you depend on My resources, the more you can celebrate My Majesty. In whatever you do, consciously rely on My help—living in the joyous wonder of self-forgetfulness. As you look to Me continually for all you need, your face will reflect the Light of My surpassing Glory.

But you are a chosen generation, a royal priesthood, a holy nation, His own special people, that you may proclaim the praises of Him who called you out of darkness into His marvelous light.

1 PETER 2:9 NKJV

I delight greatly in the LORD; my soul rejoices in my God. For he has clothed me with garments of salvation and arrayed me in a robe of righteousness, as a bridegroom adorns his head like a priest, and as a bride adorns herself with her jewels.

ISAIAH 61:10

"I am the vine, you are the branches. He who abides in Me, and I in him, bears much fruit; for without Me you can do nothing."

JOHN 15:5 NKJV

And we, who with unveiled faces all reflect the Lord's glory, are being transformed into his likeness with ever-increasing glory, which comes from the Lord, who is the Spirit.

2 CORINTHIANS 3:18

THE FUTURE

I KNOW THE PLANS I HAVE FOR YOU, PLANS TO PROSPER YOU AND NOT TO HARM YOU, PLANS TO GIVE YOU HOPE AND A FUTURE. This promise provides a feast of encouragement—offering you prosperity, hope, and a blessed future. Because the world is so fractured and full of pain, people tend to think dark thoughts and feel hopeless about the future. Unless you stay alert, you are vulnerable to such thoughts and feelings too. This makes you easy prey for *your adversary, the devil, who prowls about like a roaring lion, seeking someone to devour*. I gave My body on the cross to provide eternal nourishment for you, but the evil one wants to devour you! The contrast is crystal-clear, and the stakes are immeasurably high.

Mankind has a voracious appetite for finding out what the future will bring. Astrologers and fortune-tellers capitalize on this lust to peer into *secret things—things that belong to Me*. However, to feast on Me you must live in the present moment. This is where you can encounter Me and enjoy My Presence. As you come to the table of My delights, be sure to bring your fork of trust and your spoon of thankfulness. Take plenty of time enjoying Me, and your *soul will delight in the richest of fare*.

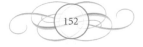

"I know the plans I have for you," declares the LORD,
"plans to prosper you and not to harm you, plans
to give you hope and a future."

JEREMIAH 29:11

Be of sober spirit, be on the alert.
Your adversary, the devil, prowls around like
a roaring lion, seeking someone to devour.

1 PETER 5:8 NASB

The secret things belong to the LORD our God,
but those things which are revealed belong to us
and to our children forever, that we may
do all the words of this law.

DEUTERONOMY 29:29 NKJV

"Why spend money on what is not bread,
and your labor on what does not satisfy? Listen,
listen to me, and eat what is good, and your
soul will delight in the richest of fare."

ISAIAH 55:2

TRIALS

WITH ME ALL THINGS ARE POSSIBLE. When you bump into massive difficulties on your life-path, I want you to *consider it pure Joy*. As you bounce off these "impossibilities," *My everlasting arms* are wide open—ready to catch you, calm you, and help you do what does not seem possible. You can be joyful in the midst of perplexing problems because I am *God your Savior*. I have already accomplished the greatest miracle—saving you from your sins. If you keep looking to Me, your resurrected Lord and King, your pessimism will eventually yield to courage. Though you are an earthbound creature in many ways, your soul shares in My eternal victory.

Since I am infinite, "impossibilities" are My specialty. I delight in them because they display My Glory so vividly. They also help you live the way I intended: in joyful, trusting dependence on Me. The next time you face an "impossible" situation, turn to Me immediately with a hopeful heart. Acknowledge your total inadequacy, and cling to Me—relying on My infinite sufficiency. *All things are possible with Me!*

Jesus looked at them and said, "With man this is impossible, but with God all things are possible."
MATTHEW 19:26

Consider it pure joy, my brothers, when you face trials of many kinds, because you know that the testing of your faith develops perseverance.
JAMES 1:2–3

The eternal God is your refuge, and underneath are the everlasting arms.
DEUTERONOMY 33:27 NKJV

Though the fig tree does not bud and there are no grapes on the vines, though the olive crop fails and the fields produce no food, though there are no sheep in the pen and no cattle in the stalls, yet I will rejoice in the LORD, I will be joyful in God my Savior.
HABAKKUK 3:17–18

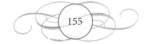

STRIVING

To receive My Peace, you must change your grasping, controlling stance to one of openness and trust. Grasping and controlling are your means of trying to feel safe. However, such an approach actually hurts you and works against you: The more you manipulate and maneuver for control, the more anxious you become.

Rather than striving for peace of mind through these means, abandon yourself to Me. My hand is the only thing you can grasp without damaging your soul. Let Me help you open your hands and receive all that I have for you.

What you do with your body can help or hinder what goes on in your soul. When you realize you are grasping for control, become aware of your body language. Intentionally open your hands, releasing your concerns to Me and inviting Me to take charge. Open your heart and mind as well, as you lift your hands to Me. You are now in a good position to receive My many blessings, not the least of which is awareness of My Presence.

Enjoy the Peace that flows out from Me while you bask in the Light of My Love. Then, when you move

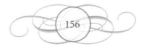

156

back into your activities, consciously grasp My hand in childlike dependence. *For I am the Lord your God, who takes hold of your right hand and says to you, "Do not fear; I will help you."*

I want men everywhere to lift up holy hands in prayer, without anger or disputing.
1 TIMOTHY 2:8

On the evening of that first day of the week, when the disciples were together, with the doors locked for fear of the Jews, Jesus came and stood among them and said, "Peace be with you!"
JOHN 20:19

Therefore whoever humbles himself as this little child is the greatest in the kingdom of heaven.
MATTHEW 18:4 NKJV

For I am the LORD, your God, who takes hold of your right hand and says to you, Do not fear; I will help you.
ISAIAH 41:13

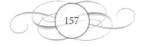

ASSURANCE

TRUTH IS THE VERY HEART OF WHO I AM, SO YOU CANNOT LOVE ME WITHOUT LOVING THE TRUTH. *In fact, for this reason I came into the world, to testify to the truth.* I abhor lies—especially about salvation, which is *through Me* alone. In this age of "tolerance," many people deem it arrogant to believe in absolute truth. However, unless the gospel is absolutely true, it is not good news at all. If it is only partially true, people who trust Me as Savior *are to be pitied more than all men.*

Both My words and My works *testify to the truth.* I performed countless *miraculous signs* so that the display of My Glory would confirm the truth of My teaching. My resurrection and ascension further verify that I am who I claim to be: the only true Savior-God.

I want you to build your life on My transcendent truth. As you *listen to Me*—through My Word and My Spirit—your life gains meaning and purpose. You can face each day with confidence: secure in My eternal Love, embracing challenges as adventures to share with Me. The more you build your life on the truth, the closer to Me you can live—enjoying Me, depending on Me, glorifying Me.

Jesus said to him, "I am the way, the truth, and the life. No one comes to the Father except through Me."

JOHN 14:6

"You are a king, then!" said Pilate. Jesus answered, "You are right. . . . In fact, for this reason I was born, and for this I came into the world, to testify to the truth. Everyone on the side of truth listens to Me."

JOHN 18:37

If only for this life we have hope in Christ, we are to be pitied more than all men.

1 CORINTHIANS 15:19

Jesus did many other miraculous signs in the presence of his disciples, which are not recorded in this book. But these are written that you may believe that Jesus is the Christ, the Son of God, and that by believing you may have life in his name.

JOHN 20:30–31

INTIMACY WITH HIM

I—THE ETERNAL LOVER OF YOUR SOUL—
DESIRE INTIMATE CONNECTION WITH YOU.
When you seek to know Me more fully, this brings Me
much pleasure. My knowledge of you is unlimited: I
know everything about you, and I choose to love you
ardently in spite of your imperfections. I have already
paid the penalty for all the things in your life—past,
present, and future—that could isolate you from Me.

Though there is still some darkness in your heart,
the Light of the knowledge of My Glory continues
shining within you—*as a Light that shines in a dark
place, until the day dawns and the morning star rises
in your heart.* Your part in this unfolding drama is to
wait trustingly in My holy Presence. This is the most
effective way to develop a more intimate relationship
with Me. Though waiting can be a difficult discipline,
the blessings far outweigh your effort. Moreover, the
effort *itself* can bless you, because it keeps you focusing on Me. As you wait in the Light of My Presence,
My Love falls steadily upon you. In this brilliant Love-
Light you can sometimes catch glimpses of *the Glory
revealed in My Face.*

*For all have sinned and fall short of the glory of God,
and are justified freely by his grace through the
redemption that came by Christ Jesus.*

ROMANS 3:23–24

*For God, who said, "Let light shine out of darkness,"
made His light shine in our hearts to give us the light of
the knowledge of the glory of God in the face of Christ.*

2 CORINTHIANS 4:6

*And so we have the prophetic word confirmed,
which you do well to heed as a light that shines
in a dark place, until the day dawns and the
morning star rises in your hearts.*

2 PETER 1:19 NKJV

*I wait for the LORD, my soul waits, and in his word I
put my hope. My soul waits for the Lord more
than watchmen wait for the morning . . .*

PSALM 130:5–6

PLEASING HIM

I BLESS YOU AND KEEP YOU; I MAKE MY FACE SHINE UPON YOU; I TURN MY FACE TOWARD YOU AND GIVE YOU PEACE. I want you to meditate on this blessing, for it expresses well the overflow of My heart toward you. I long to bless My children, but so often they are unwilling to come to Me and linger in My loving Presence. They turn primarily to lesser gods: people, wealth, success. You are not immune to such idolatry, but you do have some bright moments of seeking Me first and foremost. Since you have *tasted and seen that I am good*, your appetite for Me is steadily improving.

Deep within the human heart lies intense longing for My approval. Many people hate Me because they fear My disapproval. They know instinctively they have broken My laws, so they try to live as far from Me as possible. They fail to recognize My universal Presence: There is no place in the universe where I am not present. How tragic that so many try to run from Me, rather than come—believing—for Life! Those who *do* come to Me discover that *My yoke is easy and My burden is light*. Like you, they find not only My approval but also *rest for their souls*. While I am blessing you with soul-rest, I graciously *give you Peace*.

162

*"The LORD bless you and keep you; the LORD make his
face shine upon you and be gracious to you; the LORD
turn his face toward you and give you peace."*

NUMBERS 6:24–26

*Oh, taste and see that the LORD is good; blessed
is the man who trusts in Him!*

PSALM 34:8 NKJV

*For my Father's will is that everyone who looks to the
Son and believes in him shall have eternal life, and
I will raise him up at the last day.*

JOHN 6:40

*"Come to me, all you who are weary and burdened,
and I will give you rest. Take my yoke upon you and
learn from me, for I am gentle and humble in heart,
and you will find rest for your souls. For my
yoke is easy and my burden is light."*

MATTHEW 11:28–30

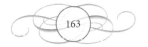

FEAR

I MYSELF GO BEFORE YOU—OPENING UP THE
WAY. *I will never leave you nor forsake you.* Therefore,
you need not be afraid or discouraged. I realize,
though, that feelings often fail to submit to logic. So
don't be surprised when your emotions rebel against
your will. David—who was both a mighty warrior and
a gifted poet—expressed fearfulness, trembling, and
even overwhelming horror in one of his psalms. Yet his
trust in Me was genuine and deep. His life and his writing demonstrate that fear does not "trump" trust: They
can coexist. This is why David could proclaim, "When
I am afraid, I will trust in You."

Trust is a relational word. It's one of the prime
ways you can draw near Me. When you are afraid,
don't blame yourself for having that very human emotion. Instead, acknowledge what you are feeling; then
affirm your trust in Me—out loud or in a whisper. This
affirmation protects you from the lie that feeling fearful means you don't trust Me. Even better, it brings you
consciously into My Presence, where you can find comfort and hope. The Light of My Presence illuminates
the vast dimensions of My Love for you—empowering
you *to grasp how wide and long and high and deep My
Love is, and to know this Love that surpasses knowledge.*

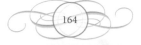

The Lord himself goes before you and will be with you; he will never leave you nor forsake you. Do not be afraid; do not be discouraged.

DEUTERONOMY 31:8

Fearfulness and trembling have come upon me, and horror has overwhelmed me.

PSALM 55:5 NKJV

When I am afraid, I will trust in you.

PSALM 56:3

[I pray that you] may have power, together with all the saints, to grasp how wide and long and high and deep is the love of Christ, and to know this love that surpasses knowledge—that you may be filled to the measure of all the fullness of God.

EPHESIANS 3:18–19

ABIDING IN HIM

I AM YOUR STRENGTH AND YOUR SHIELD. When you trust in Me—My awesome strength and shielding protection—*you are helped* enormously. Weights of worry fall off you as you connect with Me through trust. The resulting lightness within you invites Joy to rush in, and you can bask in My merry Light. I have told you that *whoever follows Me will never walk in darkness, but will have the Light of Life.* An excellent way to stay near Me is to place your confidence fully in Me. A heart that trusts in Me can even *leap for Joy!*

Another good way to follow Me closely is to give thanks in every situation. One of the simplest—yet most effective—prayers is, "Thank You, Jesus." I encourage you to express your thankfulness in a variety of ways: If you are artistic, you can express yourself through singing, dancing, painting, sculpting. If you're verbally gifted, you can speak or write praises to Me. More profoundly, you can learn to worship Me *in everything* you do. *Whatever you do, do it heartily—as to Me, your Lord.* Devote yourself to thanking and praising Me; these delightful disciplines glorify Me and fill you with gladness.

*The LORD is my strength and my shield; my heart trusts
in him, and I am helped. My heart leaps for joy and
I will give thanks to him in song.*

PSALM 28:7

*When Jesus spoke again to the people, he said, "I am
the light of the world. Whoever follows me will never
walk in darkness, but will have the light of life."*

JOHN 8:12

*Rejoice always, pray without ceasing, in everything give
thanks; for this is the will of God in Christ Jesus for you.*

1 THESSALONIANS 5:16–18 NKJV

*And whatever you do, do it heartily, as to
the Lord and not to men.*

COLOSSIANS 3:23 NKJV

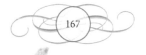

HIS PRESENCE

I WANT YOU TO SPEND TIME WITH ME FOR THE PURE PLEASURE OF BEING IN MY COMPANY. When you take delight in My Presence, you experience a foretaste of the eternal pleasures I have prepared for you. Unfortunately, the "dailyness" of life tends to pull you down, and your focus on routine duties often obscures your awareness of Me.

To enjoy My companionship in all that you do, wait in My Presence while I reveal Myself to you. Put aside thoughts of tasks awaiting you as you focus pleasurably on Me. Allow awareness of My Presence to become imprinted on your consciousness. Then move gently from this contemplative time into your routine duties and continue communing with Me, asking Me to be vibrantly involved in your work.

Having already connected with Me at a deep level, you can find Me more easily in the midst of your activities. Naturally, you will lose sight of Me at times; I know you're only human. But you can reconnect readily by moving toward Me in your thoughts, words, and feelings. The more you include Me in your awareness, the brighter your day will be: Your routines will sparkle with the liveliness of My company.

I wait for the LORD, my soul waits, and in his word I put my hope. My soul waits for the Lord more than watchmen wait for the morning, more than watchmen wait for the morning.

PSALM 130:5–6

As a father has compassion on his children, so the LORD has compassion on those who fear him; for he knows how we are formed, he remembers that we are dust.

PSALM 103:13–14

"For in him we live and move and have our being." As some of your own poets have said, "We are his offspring."

ACTS 17:28

RENEWING YOUR MIND

PEOPLE OFTEN CONSIDER THOUGHTS TO BE FLEETING AND WORTHLESS, BUT YOURS ARE SO PRECIOUS TO ME THAT I READ EACH ONE. My ability to read your every thought may be disconcerting to you. You're able to interact with other people while keeping your secret thoughts to yourself, but not so with Me! However, since secretiveness breeds loneliness, isn't it a relief that there is Someone from whom you cannot hide? Moreover, the fact that I care about every aspect of you—even all your thoughts—demonstrates how important you are to Me.

I know how difficult it is for you to control what courses through your brain. Your mind is a battleground, and evil spirits work tirelessly to influence your thinking. Your own sinfulness also finds ample expression in your thought life. You need to stay alert and fight against evil! I fought and died for you, so remember who you are and Whose you are—putting on the helmet of salvation with confidence. This helmet not only protects your mind, it also reminds you of the victory I secured for you on the cross.

Because you are My treasure, I notice and rejoice as soon as your thinking turns My way. The more

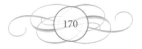

thoughts you bring to Me, the more you can share in My Joy. I disarm evil thoughts and render them powerless. Then I help you think about things that are *true, noble, right, pure, lovely, admirable—excellent and praiseworthy things*. Ponder these things while resting in the Peace of My Presence.

O LORD, you have searched me and you know me. You know when I sit and when I rise; you perceive my thoughts from afar.
PSALM 139:1–2

Take the helmet of salvation and the sword of the Spirit, which is the word of God.
EPHESIANS 6:17

Whatever is true, whatever is noble, whatever is right, whatever is pure, whatever is lovely, whatever is admirable—if anything is excellent or praiseworthy—think about such things.
PHILIPPIANS 4:8

RIGHT LIVING

I AM YOUR LIVING REDEEMER. Even *after your skin has been destroyed, you will see Me in your flesh—with your own eyes.* Before you knew Me, you were *a slave to sin.* In order to redeem you—to deliver you from this bondage—I paid the full penalty for your sins. The price was astronomical: the sacrifice of My own blood! So now you belong to Me, and you will live with Me throughout eternity.

Since *you were bought* at such an immeasurable price, I want you to *glorify Me in your body and in your spirit.* You glorify Me in your body by taking good care of yourself and abstaining from immorality. Your life is a precious gift from Me, and I want you to live it fully—in ways that bring Me Glory and give you healthy pleasure. You glorify Me in your spirit by delighting in Me above all else. This is a most joyful pursuit! The world contains much beauty and many sources of enjoyment, but I outshine them all. As you orient your spirit toward Me, I bless you with the Joy of My Presence. This pleasure is independent of your circumstances; it flows from the fountain of My eternal Love. Because you are My redeemed one, *I take great delight in you. I quiet you with My Love; I rejoice over you with singing!*

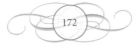

*I know that my Redeemer lives, and that in
the end he will stand upon the earth. And after my
skin has been destroyed, yet in my flesh I will see God;
I myself will see him with my own eyes . . .*

JOB 19:25–27

*Jesus replied, "I tell you the truth,
everyone who sins is a slave to sin."*

JOHN 8:34

*For you were bought at a price; therefore glorify God
in your body and in your spirit, which are God's.*

1 CORINTHIANS 6:20 NKJV

*The LORD your God is with you, he is mighty to save.
He will take great delight in you, he will quiet you with
his love, he will rejoice over you with singing.*

ZEPHANIAH 3:17

173

FAITH

WITHOUT FAITH IT IS IMPOSSIBLE TO PLEASE ME. This may seem obvious, but there are actually many people who try to approach Me without truly believing I exist. Some people simply want to cover all their bases, so they toss up an occasional prayer to Me—just in case I might really exist and someday be their Judge. Others cry out to Me at times of extreme distress and then forget about Me when the crisis is over. This is not genuine faith, and it does not please Me at all. Faith that pleases Me is much more substantial: It *perceives as real fact what is not revealed to the senses.*

I enjoy *rewarding those who earnestly seek Me.* I don't expect perfection in your search for Me, because *I remember that you are dust.* I do, however, rejoice in your seeking Me persistently—day in and day out. This is extremely pleasing to Me, and I reward you in numerous ways: I whet your appetite to know Me ever more intimately. I gradually change the desires of your heart so they line up more and more with the contents of My heart. When you are going through tough times, I pour out upon you tender, overflowing Love. As you open your heart to receive this Love-flow, you are ravishingly pleasing to Me.

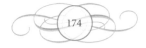

And without faith it is impossible to please God, because
anyone who comes to him must believe that he exists
and that he rewards those who earnestly seek him.

HEBREWS 11:6

Now faith is the assurance (the confirmation,
the title deed) of the things [we] hope for, being
the proof of things [we] do not see and the conviction
of their reality [faith perceiving as real fact what
is not revealed to the senses].

HEBREWS 11:1 AMP

And you will seek Me and find Me, when
you search for Me with all your heart.

JEREMIAH 29:13 NKJV

For He knows our frame;
He remembers that we are dust.

PSALM 103:14 NKJV

CONTROL

GLORIFYING AND ENJOYING ME IS A HIGHER
PRIORITY THAN MAINTAINING A TIDY, STRUC-
TURED LIFE. Your heart resonates with this truth,
but in practice, you usually strive to keep things under
control. I read your thoughts with perfect accuracy, so
I know how easily you lose perspective. When "order"
becomes your focus, you often try to enlist My help in
getting control of your circumstances.

Let's think together about this: To glorify and
enjoy Me as you desire, you need to relinquish control to Me. You may feel as if this would involve giving
up something valuable, because controlling things is a
way you try to feel safe. In reality, however, what I'm
asking you to give up—the striving to maintain control—is something that frustrates you far more than it
helps you. Even if you succeed in creating a tidy life for
a time, you will not be able to maintain it.

Instead of wasting your energy on an impossible
task, endeavor to celebrate your relationship with
Me. Learn to *walk more consistently in the Light of My
Presence*. Indeed, those who walk in this Light can
rejoice in Me all day long, exulting in My righteousness.
Glorify Me by living joyously in My energizing Light.

*I have brought you glory on earth by completing
the work you gave me to do. And now, Father, glorify
me in your presence with the glory I had with
you before the world began.*

JOHN 17:4–5

*O LORD, you have searched me and you know me.
You know when I sit and when I rise; you
perceive my thoughts from afar.*

PSALM 139:1–2

*Blessed are those who have learned to acclaim
you, who walk in the light of your presence, O LORD.
They rejoice in your name all day long;
they exult in your righteousness.*

PSALM 89:15–16

WORSHIP

I AM THE SUN OF RIGHTEOUSNESS, GLORIOUSLY BRILLIANT AND WORTHY OF ALL ADORATION. There is *healing in My wings and My beams* of Glory-Light. Wait with Me while My healing Presence shines brightly upon and within you. Open your soul to receive the full spectrum of these Glory-beams. Let My living Light energize you so bountifully that you go out from this waiting time *like a calf released from its stall, leaping for Joy!*

My promises are ripe with abundant blessings, but they are not for everyone. Only those who *revere and worshipfully fear My Name* will receive the promised benefits. Many people casually abuse My Name, using it as a cheap swearword. This is blasphemy, and it carries serious consequences. Blasphemers cannot expect to receive favor from Me unless they repent. I want all people to revere My Name—regarding it as sacred because it represents Me, *the King of Glory*. Since you *do* honor My Name, you are free to enjoy the good things I have promised: healing in the intimacy of My Presence, exuberant Joy that cannot be contained, and much more. As you bask in these delightful blessings, remember to tell others about your glorious King.

Then they also can become worshipers who revere Me
and praise My holy Name.

*But unto you who revere and worshipfully fear My
name shall the Sun of Righteousness arise with healing
in His wings and His beams, and you shall go forth . . .
like calves [released] from the stall and leap for joy.*
MALACHI 4:2 AMP

*You shall not misuse the name of the
LORD your God, for the LORD will not hold anyone
guiltless who misuses his name.*
EXODUS 20:7

*Lift up your heads, O you gates! And be lifted up, you
everlasting doors! And the King of glory shall come in.*
PSALM 24:7 NKJV

HIS LOVE

MY LOVE GOES ON AND ON INTO THE FUTURE-GLORY OF FOREVER. I am the mysterious Lover who will *never* let you go. Many people despise mystery, because they want to reduce life to what they can comprehend through their senses and reasoning. This is like trying to love someone by spending time with the person's picture rather than with the living human being. Love is both mysterious and sacred because it is the essence of the perfect relationships We enjoy within the Trinity. It is also how I—your living Savior—choose to relate to *you*. There is no barrier between us because *My blood keeps on cleansing you from all sin*. So you are free to *draw near Me*; in response, I come closer to you.

A blessed way to come near Me is to ponder the strength of My Love: *Many waters cannot quench it; rivers cannot wash it away*. This Love is the most powerful force in the universe, and it will ultimately prevail—in your current life (as you trust Me) and throughout eternity. Remember that you are *My beloved*; this is your forever-identity. Rejoice in this intimate security, for it is worth more than all the wealth in the world!

But if we walk in the Light as He Himself is in the Light, we have fellowship with one another, and the blood of Jesus His Son cleanses us from all sin.

1 JOHN 1:7 NASB

Draw near to God and He will draw near to you.

JAMES 4:8 NKJV

Many waters cannot quench love; rivers cannot wash it away. If one were to give all the wealth of his house for love, it would be utterly scorned.

SONG OF SONGS 8:7

And so we know and rely on the love God has for us. God is love. Whoever lives in love lives in God, and God in him. In this way, love is made complete among us so that we will have confidence on the day of judgment, because in this world we are like him. There is no fear in love. But perfect love drives out fear.

1 JOHN 4:16–18

IDOLATRY

MY EYES RANGE THROUGHOUT THE EARTH TO STRENGTHEN THOSE WHOSE HEARTS ARE FULLY COMMITTED TO ME. In this world of "spin" and outright lies, I assure you that My eyes see everything with perfect clarity. Of course, that means I also see everything about *you*. The human heart—in its fallen condition—*is deceitful above all things*. Idol-making comes naturally to all people, including My followers. Even good things can become idols if they slither into first place in your heart. Nonetheless, your longing for a heart *fully committed to Me* makes you teachable. When My Spirit points out an idol, you confess it as sin and turn back to Me: *your First Love*. In response, I strengthen you—empowering you to live for Me more and more. Thus, as we work together, your heart becomes increasingly devoted to Me.

If you cringe at the thought of My seeing everything about you, remember that I look at you through eyes of grace. Though nothing is hidden from My sight, I choose to view you through grace-vision: I see you radiantly attired in *garments of salvation,* and this is a glorious sight! Look up to Me; let the approving Love in My eyes strengthen and delight you.

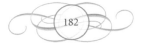

*For the eyes of the LORD range throughout
the earth to strengthen those whose hearts
are fully committed to Him . . .*
2 CHRONICLES 16:9

*The heart is deceitful above all things, and
desperately wicked; who can know it?*
JEREMIAH 17:9 NKJV

*Nevertheless I have this against you,
that you have left your first love.*
REVELATION 2:4 NKJV

*I delight greatly in the LORD; my soul rejoices in my
God. For he has clothed me with garments of
salvation and arrayed me in a robe of righteousness,
as a bridegroom adorns his head like a priest,
and as a bride adorns herself with her jewels.*
ISAIAH 61:10

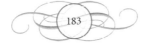

TRUST

HAVE NO FEAR OF BAD NEWS. I want your heart to be *steadfast, trusting in Me—in My unfailing Love.* Remember that My Love for you is independent of your performance. So, when you become anxious or fearful, I do not love you less. Having a steadfast heart is an excellent goal, and you are making some progress in this quest. I am like a proud parent watching his baby learn to walk, eager to see you take each step of trust—however small. No matter how unsteadily you walk, I applaud each trust-step as if it were an Olympic feat. When you stumble or fall, I give you time to pull yourself back up. However, if you lift your arms to Me, seeking My help, I cannot resist coming to your aid.

Looking to Me for help demonstrates genuine trust in Me. It is easy to turn against yourself when you have failed, but this is not pleasing to Me. Some of My children blame others—or Me—for their failures. All of these responses are hurtful and counterproductive. The sooner you turn toward Me, the better. My tender Love can soothe your wounded pride and help you learn from your mistakes. As you sit in ashes of failure, looking up to Me, you grow more humble. You realize that you need Me continually to develop

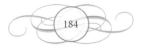

a steadfast heart. *In My unfailing Love I will lead you. In My strength I will guide you*—all the way *to My holy dwelling.*

He will have no fear of bad news; his heart is steadfast, trusting in the LORD.
PSALM 112:7

Let the morning bring me word of your unfailing love, for I have put my trust in you. Show me the way I should go, for to you I lift up my soul.
PSALM 143:8

To console those who mourn in Zion, to give them beauty for ashes, the oil of joy for mourning, the garment of praise for the spirit of heaviness; . . . that He may be glorified.
ISAIAH 61:3 NKJV

In your unfailing love you will lead the people you have redeemed. In your strength you will guide them to your holy dwelling.
EXODUS 15:13

DEPENDING ON HIM

GO GENTLY THROUGH THE DAY, LEANING ON ME AND ENJOYING MY PRESENCE. I say *gently*, not only because it is the best way for you to cope with the demands of the day, but because I Myself am gentle—especially with those who are weak. You need to lean on someone, and I am definitely the most reliable Person you could ever find. I—the Lord of the universe—am always available to help you.

My availability is based on My commitment to you, which is deeper and stronger than even the most ardent wedding vows. No matter how passionately in love a bride and groom may be, their vows last only until one of them dies. My commitment, however, is absolutely unlimited. When you asked Me to be your Savior, I wed you for eternity. *Neither death nor life, nor anything else in all creation can separate you from My Love!*

I invite you to lean on Me as much as you like, but I also want you to enjoy Me. When you are weary, you find it easier to lean on Me than to enjoy My company. In an attempt to save energy, you tend to shut down emotionally. But it is possible for you to *be joyful in Me—Your Savior*—even in desperate circumstances.

Remember that *I am your strength*. Rejoice in Me, and relax while I speak to you in *gentle whispers*.

For I am convinced that neither death nor life, neither angels nor demons, neither the present nor the future, nor any powers, neither height nor depth, nor anything else in all creation, will be able to separate us from the love of God that is in Christ Jesus our Lord.

ROMANS 8:38–39

Though the fig tree does not bud and there are no grapes on the vines, though the olive crop fails and the fields produce no food, though there are no sheep in the pen and no cattle in the stalls, yet I will rejoice in the LORD, I will be joyful in God my Savior. The Sovereign LORD is my strength; he makes my feet like the feet of a deer, he enables me to go on the heights.

HABAKKUK 3:17–19

After the earthquake came a fire, but the LORD was not in the fire. And after the fire came a gentle whisper.

1 KINGS 19:12

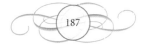

TRANSFORMATION

I LIVE IN YOU. This four-word fact exponentially changes your life and improves your prospects for all eternity! Don't worry about whether or not you are a fit home for Me. I am well-accustomed to living in unfit houses. Believers throughout the world and through all time have presented Me with a wide variety of deficient dwellings to inhabit. I joyfully move into these humble homes, and I work on renovating them from the inside. However, I refuse to dwell in people who think they are already "good enough" without Me. I have called such hypocrites *whitewashed tombs: beautiful on the outside* but putrid on the inside.

As you ponder the miraculous truth that *I live in you*, let your heart overflow with Joy. I am not a short-term tenant, indwelling you only as long as your behavior pleases Me. I have come to stay—permanently. Be aware, though, that My renovations can be quite painful at times, and I don't adhere to a forty-hour workweek. When My transforming work in you causes intense pain, cling trustingly to Me. I want you to *live by faith in the One who loved you and gave Himself for you*. Continue yielding to My renewal within you, and you will become more fully the masterpiece I designed you to be. Collaborate with Me, and live abundantly!

*I have been crucified with Christ and I
no longer live, but Christ lives in me. The life I live
in the body, I live by faith in the Son of God,
who loved me and gave himself for me.*

GALATIANS 2:20

*"Woe to you, teachers of the law and Pharisees, you
hypocrites! You are like whitewashed tombs, which look
beautiful on the outside but on the inside are full of
dead men's bones and everything unclean."*

MATTHEW 23:27

*For we are His workmanship, created in Christ Jesus
for good works, which God prepared beforehand
that we should walk in them.*

EPHESIANS 2:10 NKJV

*"The thief comes only to steal and kill and destroy; I
came that they may have life, and have it abundantly."*

JOHN 10:10 NASB

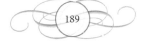

189

THANKFULNESS

A THANKFUL ATTITUDE OPENS WINDOWS OF HEAVEN THROUGH WHICH SPIRITUAL BLESS-INGS FALL FREELY. And all I require to rain those blessings on you is your gratitude! It seems such a simple choice; yet you stumble over it almost every day of your life. Let Me help you become more grateful so you can receive bountiful blessings through those openings into eternity.

As you go about your day, keep these things in mind: Throughout the Bible I repeatedly command thankfulness because it is vital to your well-being. It is also crucial for a healthy relationship with Me, since I am your Creator, your Savior, your King. When you thank Me, you acknowledge how much I have done for you. This attitude brings Joy both to you and to Me.

Giving thanks is similar to priming a pump with water so that it will produce more water. Since thankfulness is one of the spiritual blessings I bestow on you, it will increase along with the others when you "prime" Me with thanksgiving.

Remember that I am the God of all grace. When you fail in your endeavor to be thankful, simply ask Me for forgiveness. As you freely receive this priceless

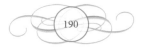

gift—thinking about what it cost Me—your gratitude will grow. Look up to Me and see spiritual blessings cascading down upon you through heaven's wide-open windows.

Enter his gates with thanksgiving and his courts with praise; give thanks to him and praise his name.
PSALM 100:4

Blessed be the God and Father of our Lord Jesus Christ, who has blessed us with every spiritual blessing in the heavenly places in Christ.
EPHESIANS 1:3 NASB

Devote yourselves to prayer, being watchful and thankful.
COLOSSIANS 4:2

Rejoice greatly, O daughter of Zion! Shout, O daughter of Jerusalem! Behold, your King is coming to you . . .
ZECHARIAH 9:9 NKJV

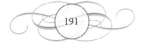

HIS PRESENCE

I WILL NEVER LEAVE YOU OR FORSAKE YOU. Many of My followers think they have to jump through all the right hoops to "stay in fellowship" with Me. If that were true, they would never be able to enjoy My Presence. They would have to be perfect to gain an audience with Me. Instead of striving to be good enough, I invite you to come confidently into My bright Presence.

If you walk in the Light as I am in the Light, My blood continually cleanses you from all sin. When you become aware of sins, I want you to confess them and seek My help in making needed changes. Nonetheless, your status with Me is not based on confessing your sins quickly enough or thoroughly enough. The only thing that keeps you right with Me is My perfect righteousness, which I gave you freely and permanently when you joined My royal family.

Walking in the Light of My Presence blesses you in many ways. Good things are better and bad things more bearable when you share them with Me. As you bask in My Love-Light, you are better able to love others and enjoy fellowship with them. You are less likely to stumble or fall, because sins are garishly obvious in My holy

Light. As you walk in this Light with Me, I encourage you to *exult in My righteousness.*

Keep your lives free from the love of money and be content with what you have, because God has said, "Never will I leave you; never will I forsake you."
HEBREWS 13:5

But if we walk in the light as He is in the light, we have fellowship with one another, and the blood of Jesus Christ His Son cleanses us from all sin.
1 JOHN 1:7 NKJV

Blessed are those who have learned to acclaim you, who walk in the light of your presence, O LORD. They rejoice in your name all day long; they exult in your righteousness.
PSALM 89:15–16

HIS FORGIVENESS

As you come to know Me more intimately, you grow increasingly aware of your sins. This presents you with a continual choice—to focus on your flaws and failures or to rejoice in My glorious gift of salvation. When My ultimate sacrifice is your focus, you live in joyful assurance of being wondrously loved. There is *no greater Love than this*, and it is yours every nanosecond of your life. The best response to such Love is to love Me with your whole being. Of course, your loving Me is not what saves you, but it *does* demonstrate your grateful awareness of how much I forgive you.

Tragically, many people think they have little—if anything—for Me to forgive. They have been deceived by the prevailing lie that there is no absolute truth. They think good and evil are relative terms; therefore, they see no need for a Savior. These deceived ones do not seek My forgiveness, so their sins are not forgiven and they have no love for Me. Their minds remain darkened by the evil one's deceptions. Only My Love-Light can penetrate that thick darkness. As you walk in the Light of My Presence let My Love flow through you to others, shining into their darkness. Because you are

My follower, you *never walk in darkness*—you *have the Light of Life!*

But I trust in your unfailing love; my heart rejoices in your salvation. I will sing to the LORD, for he has been good to me.
PSALM 13:5–6

Greater love has no one than this, than to lay down one's life for his friends.
JOHN 15:13 NKJV

Therefore, I tell you, her many sins have been forgiven—for she loved much. But he who has been forgiven little loves little.
LUKE 7:47

When Jesus spoke again to the people, he said, "I am the light of the world. Whoever follows me will never walk in darkness, but will have the light of life."
JOHN 8:12

FREEDOM IN HIM

Come to Me when you are hurting, and I will share your pain. Come to Me when you are joyful, and I will share your Joy—multiplying it many times over.

I invite you to come to Me just as you are—no matter what condition you're in. You don't have to clean up your act first, since I already know the worst about you. When you're hurting, you want to be with someone who understands you without condemning you. When you're happy, you delight in being with someone who loves you enough to celebrate with you. I understand you compassionately and love you exuberantly, so bring more and more of yourself to Me.

Most people are selective about which parts of themselves they share with Me. Some hesitate to bring Me the traits they consider shameful. Others are so used to living with painful feelings—loneliness, fear, guilt—that it never occurs to them to ask for help in dealing with these things. Still others get so preoccupied with their struggles that they forget I'm even here.

There are hurting parts of you that I desire to heal. However, some of them have been with you so long that you consider them part of your identity. You carry

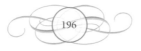

them with you wherever you go, with little awareness. On occasions when you have brought some damaged portion of yourself to Me, I have helped you walk in newfound freedom. However, you are so addicted to certain painful patterns that you cannot easily break free from them. Only repeatedly exposing them to My healing Presence will bring you long-term freedom. When that happens, you will be released to experience Joy in much fuller measure. I will share your Joy and multiply it many times over.

Therefore, there is now no condemnation
for those who are in Christ Jesus.
ROMANS 8:1

The LORD has done great things for us,
and we are filled with joy.
PSALM 126:3

In my anguish I cried to the LORD, and
he answered by setting me free.
PSALM 118:5

So if the Son sets you free, you will be free indeed.
JOHN 8:36

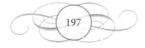

EMPTINESS

I DESIGNED YOU TO BE FILLED WITH HEAVENLY CONTENTS: MY LOVE, JOY, AND PEACE. However, you are a *frail earthen vessel*, so these contents leak out of you. Unless you are refilled—over and over again—you become increasingly empty.

I am eager to pour out My abundance upon and within you, but this takes time: focused time with Me. Come to Me and linger in My Presence. Do not rush in, trying to grab as much blessing as you can before making a quick exit. Instead, stay with Me awhile, enjoying the awesome privilege of communing with your King. As you wait with Me, My very Life streams into you, filling you up with heavenly substance.

I want you to be all Mine—overflowing with My Love, Joy, and Peace. Because these divine gifts leak out of you, you need Me continually for renewal. Your neediness is not a mistake or defect: It keeps you looking to Me, depending on Me, communicating with Me. Though you are a frail jar of clay, I have blessed you with the most *precious treasure: the divine Light of the Gospel.* Your human frailty is necessary to show that this exceedingly great Power is not from you but from Me.

I am *Christ in you, the hope of Glory.* As I fill you

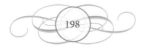

with My Glory-gifts, let My wondrous Light shine through you into other people's lives.

> *But the fruit of the Spirit is love, joy, peace,*
> *patience, kindness, goodness, faithfulness,*
> *gentleness and self-control.*
> GALATIANS 5:22–23A

> *However, we possess this precious treasure [the divine*
> *Light of the Gospel] in [frail, human] vessels of earth,*
> *that the grandeur and exceeding greatness of the power*
> *may be shown to be from God and not from ourselves.*
> 2 CORINTHIANS 4:7 AMP

> *To them God has chosen to make known among*
> *the Gentiles the glorious riches of his mystery,*
> *which is Christ in you, the hope of glory.*
> COLOSSIANS 1:27

> *In the same way, let your light shine before men,*
> *that they may see your good deeds and*
> *praise your Father in heaven.*
> MATTHEW 5:16

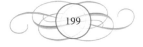

INTIMACY WITH HIM

DO NOT FEEL GUILTY ABOUT TAKING TIME TO SEEK MY FACE; YOU ARE SIMPLY RESPONDING TO THE TUGS OF DIVINITY WITHIN YOU. I made you in My image, and I hid heaven in your heart.

Much of this world's angst is actually a longing for the perfection of heaven. Blatant sin is often a misguided attempt to fill the emptiness created by that longing. *The god of this age has blinded the minds of unbelievers* so that they search for heaven in hellish ways: excesses and perversions of every kind. However, great sinners can be transformed into exceptional Christians when they turn their passionate appetites toward Me.

My Love and forgiveness satisfy soul-hunger as nothing else can, so it is good that you yearn for more than this world can provide. You were not designed to find total satisfaction in the here-and-now, because you were crafted in My image.

Since heaven is My home, it is your ultimate home too, where all of your longings will be perfectly satisfied. I placed a bit of heavenly matter in your heart so you would seek Me even now for a taste of that eternal reality. Refuse to feel guilty about something that brings Me such pleasure! I delight in your seeking heart.

Look to the LORD and his strength;
seek his face always.
PSALM 105:4

The god of this age has blinded the minds of
unbelievers, so that they cannot see the light of the
gospel of the glory of Christ, who is the image of God.
2 CORINTHIANS 4:4

Why spend money on what is not bread,
and your labor on what does not satisfy? Listen,
listen to me and eat what is good, and your
soul will delight in the richest of fare.
ISAIAH 55:2

ADVERSITY

My followers must go through many hardships. Nonetheless, the gospel is amazingly *good news,* because My death as your substitute paid the full penalty for all your sins! At conversion you began a new life: one that is both an adventure and a Love-story. Adventure tales are never about predictable, easy situations. They invariably contain conflicts, adversity, defeats, and triumphs. Before I died, I warned My disciples about the *tribulation, trials, distress, and frustration* they would have in this world. Then I immediately reassured them: *I have overcome the world; I have deprived it of power to harm you and have conquered it for you.* In Me you are victorious!

Your new life is not only an adventure but also a Love-story. As you journey toward heaven, your eternal Lover never leaves your side. I share both your good times and your struggles. I embrace you in My *everlasting arms,* helping you extract good from adversity. I devise creative ways to reveal Myself to you, and I rejoice when you are attentive. While using My future-knowledge to prepare you for what is ahead, I train you to enjoy My Presence in the present. When you are struggling deeply, I offer you My Peace. At the end of

your journey, you will be able to look back and see that
hardships shared with Me are radiant treasures—full
of Love and Glory.

They preached the good news in that city and won a
large number of disciples. . . . "We must go through
many hardships to enter the kingdom of God," they said.
ACTS 14:21–22

I have told you these things, so that in Me
you may have [perfect] peace and confidence.
In the world you have tribulation and trials and
distress and frustration; but be of good cheer [take
courage; be confident, certain, undaunted]! For I have
overcome the world. [I have deprived it of power
to harm you and have conquered it for you.]
JOHN 16:33 AMP

The eternal God is your refuge, and underneath
are the everlasting arms.
DEUTERONOMY 33:27 NKJV

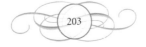

RESTING IN HIM

STAND AT THE CROSSROADS AND LOOK; ASK FOR THE ANCIENT PATHS, ASK WHERE THE GOOD WAY IS, AND WALK IN IT. In order to walk in the good way, you need to *be alert: praying in the Spirit on all occasions*. With My Spirit's help you can recognize a crossroads when you come upon it, instead of rushing past the choice-point without even noticing. If you are unsure which way to go, pause and wait with Me. Stay in communication with Me while you're standing and looking. Trust Me to show you the way forward in My timing.

If you follow these instructions, you will not only *walk in the good way;* you will also *find rest for your soul.* I know how weary you are and how desperately you need soul-rest. Even when your body is still, your thoughts tend to go hither and yon. If you want My help in taming those thoughts, bring them to Me. I already know what you're thinking, so you have nothing to hide. You need to wait in My Presence, giving Me time to help you think My thoughts. Though you may feel as if you're wasting time, you are actually doing the opposite. Your steps will be fewer but you will accomplish much more, for you will be staying close to

Me—*the Way, the Truth, and the Life.* No matter how strenuous your journey, you can find soul-rest in My company.

This is what the LORD says: "Stand at the crossroads and look; ask for the ancient paths, ask where the good way is, and walk in it, and you will find rest for your souls."
JEREMIAH 6:16

And pray in the Spirit on all occasions with all kinds of prayers and requests. With this in mind, be alert and always keep on praying for all the saints.
EPHESIANS 6:18

Jesus said to him, "I am the way, the truth, and the life. No one comes to the Father except through Me."
JOHN 14:6 NKJV

BROKENNESS

I AM THE GOD OF DIVINE REVERSALS. I CAN GLEAN GOOD OUT OF EVIL: MY MASTER PLAN BRINGS VICTORY OUT OF APPARENT DEFEAT. Come to Me just as you are—wounded from battle—and expose your wounds to My healing Light. You need to spend ample time with Me, opening yourself fully to My living Presence. Many people who are seriously ill have been successfully treated by being placed outdoors in sunlight and fresh air for hours at a time. Similarly, you need substantial amounts of time soaking in the Light of My Presence so I can heal your deep wounds.

When you experience a divine reversal in your life, you are thrilled to observe how masterfully I operate in the world. Your suffering gains meaning because you know I can—and do—bring good out of evil. Ultimately, My plans will not be thwarted. *I* have the last word! As you see how utterly beyond you are My wisdom and ways, you get a glimpse of My Glory. This inspires you to worship Me—bowing before My infinite intelligence and limitless Power. As you open your soul to Me in worship, you gain assurance of My unfailing Love. *I know the plans I have for you: plans to prosper you and not to harm you, plans to give you hope and a future.*

"And as for you, you meant evil against me, but God meant it for good in order to bring about this present result, to preserve many people alive."

GENESIS 50:20 NASB

For as the heavens are higher than the earth, so are My ways higher than your ways, and My thoughts than your thoughts.

ISAIAH 55:9 NKJV

May your unfailing love rest upon us, O LORD, even as we put our hope in you.

PSALM 33:22

"For I know the plans I have for you," declares the LORD, "plans to prosper you and not to harm you, plans to give you hope and a future."

JEREMIAH 29:1

DESIRING HIM

I AM PLEASED THAT YOU ARE ZEALOUS TO KNOW ME. Seeking to *understand Me* is like standing at the edge of a glorious ocean, trying to absorb its vast beauty—yet knowing you can see only a tiny portion of the waters stretching out before you. It's good that you realize what a small portion of My infinite greatness you can actually comprehend. This awareness is an invitation to worship Me—humbly rejoicing in My boundless Glory. Though your understanding of Me is so limited, there are no bounds to your enjoyment of Me!

I reveal Myself to you in countless ways, because of My deep desire for you to know Me. The Bible graphically describes My unrestrained eagerness to connect with My children. The prophet Isaiah pictures Me saying *"Here am I, here am I"*—*spreading out My hands all day long to a rebellious people.* In the parable of the lost son, the father (God) didn't wait for his wayward child to return home repentantly. Instead, he sacrificed his dignity and ran to his son *while he was still a long way off, fell on his neck and kissed him.* Your zeal to know Me pales in light of My ardor to reveal Myself—My Love—to you. Receive this unearned, endless Love with trembling Joy.

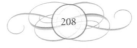

*Yes, let us know (recognize, be acquainted with,
and understand) Him; let us be zealous to know the
Lord [to appreciate, give heed to, and cherish Him]. His
going forth is prepared and certain as the dawn,
and He will come to us . . .*

HOSEA 6:3 AMP

*I permitted Myself to be sought by those who did not ask
for Me; I permitted Myself to be found by those who did
not seek Me. I said, 'Here am I, here am I,' To a nation
which did not call on My name. I have spread out My
hands all day long to a rebellious people, Who walk in
the way which is not good, following their own thoughts.*

ISAIAH 65:1–2 NASB

*And he arose and came to his father.
But when he was still a great way off, his
father saw him and had compassion, and ran
and fell on his neck and kissed him.*

LUKE 15:20 NKJV

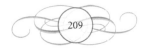

209

TRANSFORMATION

I AM YOUR LAMP; I TURN YOUR DARKNESS INTO LIGHT. Transforming you is delightful to Me. Only I know the full measure of your capabilities, and I work ceaselessly to help you become all I created you to be. My brilliant Light—in which *there is no darkness at all*—enables you to see areas where you need to change. When My Spirit spotlights an area of sin, you face a choice: You can withdraw from Me into the darkness of denial, or you can come more fully into the radiance of My Presence. If you face your sin head-on, it diminishes in power. You gain strength to walk in *My* ways—on fresh paths illuminated by My Light.

I help you deal with *all* your darkness—not only within you but also around you. Because you live in a broken world, you encounter darkness every day of your life. You inhabit a rebellious planet that screams obscene lies about who I am. This is why living close to Me—aware of My Presence—is so vital to your well-being. An excellent way to draw near Me is to change your thinking from a monologue to a dialogue: Make more and more of your thoughts a conversation with Me. When you encounter darkness in your world, talk with Me about it. I will help you see matters from My perspective, thus turning your darkness into Light.

Remember that *nothing is impossible with Me.* In fact, *with My help you can scale a wall!*

You are my lamp, O Lord; the Lord turns my darkness into light. With Your help I can advance against a troop; with my God I can scale a wall.
2 SAMUEL 22:29–30

This is the message which we have heard from Him and declare to you, that God is light and in Him is no darkness at all.
1 JOHN 1:5 NKJV

For nothing is impossible with God.
LUKE 1:37

HIS PRESENCE

I AM ALWAYS BEFORE YOU, BECKONING YOU ON—ONE STEP AT A TIME. *Neither height nor depth, nor anything else in all creation, can separate you from My loving Presence.*

I want you to live your life focused on My Presence in the present. Since you know I am always with you—leading and encouraging you—you can live in that reality moment by moment. Your mind tends to leap over the present moment to the next task, ignoring the one that is before you and the One who is before you. During rare times when you are able to stay focused on Me, your work is infused with My Presence. It is no longer laborious but delightful: more like play than work.

Living in collaboration with Me can be a foretaste of heaven. It is wonderful, though not easy: It requires a level of spiritual and mental concentration that is extremely challenging. In the Psalms, David wrote about this collaborative way of living, declaring that *he had set Me always before him.* As a shepherd, he had plenty of time to seek My Face and enjoy My Presence. He discovered the beauty of days lived with Me always before him—and beside him. I am training you to live this way too. This endeavor requires more persistent effort than anything else you have attempted. Yet, rather than detracting from your other activities, it fills them with vibrant Life.

Whatever you do, do it for Me—with Me, through Me, in Me. Even menial tasks glow with the Joy of My Presence when you do them for Me. Ultimately, nothing will be able to separate you from Me, so this you-and-I-together venture can continue throughout eternity.

For I am convinced that neither death nor life, neither angels nor demons, neither the present nor the future, nor any powers, neither height nor depth, nor anything else in all creation, will be able to separate us from the love of God that is in Christ Jesus our Lord.

ROMANS 8:38–39

I have set the LORD always before me. Because he is at my right hand, I will not be shaken.

PSALM 16:8

And whatever you do, do it heartily, as to the Lord and not to men . . . ; for you serve the Lord Christ.

COLOSSIANS 3:23–24 NKJV

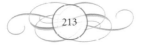

ASSURANCE

BRING YOUR ATTENTION GENTLY BACK TO ME
WHENEVER IT STARTS TO WANDER. Find relief
in the truth that I look for persistence—rather than
perfection—in your walk with Me.

Are you amazed at how quickly and how far your
mind can wander from Me? When you recognize this
has happened, don't be shattered by disappointment or
distracted by discouragement. Instead, simply return
your attention to Me and to the truth that I accept you
in all your imperfection.

Not only do I accept you as you are, I *love* you
as you are. I died a criminal's death so I could adorn
you with My own perfection. That's why bringing
your thoughts to Me is so important: It is My perfect
righteousness that saves you, and it will never be taken
away from you!

You can easily fall prey to self-rejection if you have
unrealistic expectations for yourself. When you fail, I
want you to bring focus back to Me *gently*, without judging yourself. Instead of doing further harm by
putting yourself down, persist in setting your sights on
Me. I always welcome you back with *unfailing Love*.

But when this priest had offered for all time one sacrifice
for sins, he sat down at the right hand of God. Since that
time he waits for his enemies to be made his footstool,
because by one sacrifice he has made perfect forever
those who are being made holy.

HEBREWS 10:12–14

"Martha, Martha," the Lord answered, "you are
worried and upset about many things, but only one
thing is needed. Mary has chosen what is better, and
it will not be taken away from her."

LUKE 10:41–42

How priceless is your unfailing love! Both high and low
among men find refuge in the shadow of your wings.

PSALM 36:7

WORRY

AS YOU GIVE YOURSELF MORE AND MORE TO
A LIFE OF CONSTANT COMMUNICATION WITH
ME, YOU WILL FIND THAT YOU SIMPLY HAVE
NO TIME FOR WORRY. You may be skeptical about
this statement. It seems you always find time for worrying; it's a beast you've been battling in your own
strength for years! This has been counterproductive:
The more you've tried not to worry, the more anxious you've become. So now you're worrying about
worrying!

You definitely need My help in this battle. Your
best strategy is to stop focusing on the problem and
put more energy into communicating more with Me.
This approach will help you achieve freedom from
all sorts of negative tendencies, including worry. The
idea is to replace hurtful, self-defeating behavior with
something wondrously positive—communicating
with your Creator and Savior.

Because I designed you, I know how you function
best: in rich communion with Me. As your Savior, I
also know how you function worst. But remember: I
died for every one of your sins. Don't just talk to Me;
listen to Me as well. I speak to you through My Word,

My Spirit, My creation. As you discipline yourself to communicate more with Me—*praying perseveringly*—you will find your worry-time vanishing.

Who of you by worrying can add a single hour to his life? Since you cannot do this very little thing, why do you worry about the rest?
LUKE 12:25–26

An anxious heart weighs a man down, but a kind word cheers him up.
PROVERBS 12:25

Show me your ways, O LORD, teach me your paths; guide me in your truth and teach me, for you are God my Savior, and my hope is in you all day long.
PSALM 25:4–5

Be unceasing in prayer [praying perseveringly].
1 THESSALONIANS 5:17 AMP

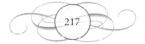

TRIALS

THOUGH I BRING GRIEF, I WILL SHOW COMPAS-SION. No matter what trials you are enduring, you can count on My Love and My compassion—neither of which will ever fail. I can bring good out of everything I allow in your life, but much of what I do is far beyond your understanding. My children often misinterpret My ways with them. When adversity strikes, they tend to feel as if I'm displeased with them. They don't realize that My most devoted followers are especially targeted in spiritual warfare. The devil and his demonic underlings delight in tormenting those who live close to Me. When you are suffering and your troubles seem endless, remember I am tenderly present in your afflictions. Instead of lamenting the way things are, search for Me in the wreckage of adversity. You will not fail to find Me *when you search for Me with all your heart.*

I want you to experience more fully the greatness of My overflowing Love. As you open yourself to My compassionate Presence, this Love flows into you more freely. Like new wine, My Love expands within you, increasing your capacity for Me. Another way to expand this capacity is to let My Love flow from you to others. I am so pleased when you do this that I flood you with more of My living Presence. As you continue this blessed adventure with Me, I fill you with ever-increasing volumes of *unfailing Love.*

Though He brings grief, He will show compassion,
so great is His unfailing Love.
LAMENTATIONS 3:32

Because of the LORD's great love we are not consumed,
for his compassions never fail. They are new
every morning; great is your faithfulness.
LAMENTATIONS 3:22–23

And you will seek Me and find Me, when you
search for Me with all your heart. I will
be found by you, says the LORD . . .
JEREMIAH 29:13–14 NKJV

TRUST

I WILL SATISFY YOUR NEEDS IN A SUN-SCORCHED LAND AND WILL STRENGTHEN YOUR FRAME. I have perfect knowledge of your body's condition. *Your frame was not hidden from Me when you were made in secret.* I handcrafted you Myself; you are *fearfully and wonderfully made!*

I am the Gardener, and you are My garden. Even when you are enduring sun-scorching trials I can *satisfy your needs* and keep you *well watered, like a spring whose waters never fail.* To receive My unfailing provisions, you need to trust Me and thank Me—no matter what.

I, your sovereign Lord, *will guide you always.* I delight in watching over you and helping you walk in My ways. Remember, though, that you also have responsibility: to follow the guidance I provide. It is essential to study My Word, for I am vibrantly present in it. The closer you live to Me, the easier it is to find and follow My path for you. This way of living is not only for guidance but also for matchless enjoyment. *I will show you the path of Life; in My Presence is fullness of Joy; at My right hand are pleasures forevermore.*

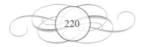

The LORD will guide you always; he will satisfy your
needs in a sun-scorched land and will strengthen
your frame. You will be like a well-watered garden,
like a spring whose waters never fail.

ISAIAH 58:11

I will praise You, for I am fearfully and wonderfully
made; marvelous are Your works, and that my soul
knows very well. My frame was not hidden from You,
when I was made in secret, and skillfully wrought
in the lowest parts of the earth.

PSALM 139:14–15 NKJV

Your word is a lamp to my feet and a light for my path.

PSALM 119:105

You will show me the path of life;
in Your presence is fullness of joy; at Your
right hand are pleasures forevermore.

PSALM 16:11 NKJV

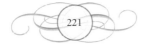

HIS SUFFICIENCY

IN UNION WITH ME YOU ARE COMPLETE. In closeness to Me you are transformed more and more into the one I designed you to be.

I know that you often feel incomplete, as if some vital part of you is missing. When this is just a feeling, not a conscious thought, you respond in many unproductive ways: comforting yourself with food, seeking entertainment, searching for yourself in the mirror, and so on. All the while I am with you, patiently waiting for you to remember Me. If you continue to go your own way—seeking satisfaction where there is none—you become increasingly frustrated. Your agitated condition makes it hard for you to turn back to Me, the only One who can complete you. But it is never too late to cry out, "Help me, Jesus!"

When a child of Mine calls out to Me, I never fail to respond. I may not provide instant relief, as if I were a genie, but I go to work immediately, setting in motion the conditions you need. I help you gain awareness of what you have been doing: seeking fulfillment in worldly ways. In response to your neediness, I offer you My glorious riches. When you have settled down enough to think clearly, I invite you to *come near Me*, where you can find completeness.

As you center your attention on Me—resting in the rarified air of My Presence —I bless you with My Peace. Though you are just a *jar of clay*, I fill you with My treasure: *the Light of the knowledge of My Glory*. This divine Light fills you to the brim—making you complete. It also transforms you, bit by bit, into the masterpiece I designed you to be.

Perseverance must finish its work so that you may be mature and complete, not lacking anything.
JAMES 1:4

He fulfills the desires of those who fear him; he hears their cry and saves them.
PSALM 145:19

Come near to God and he will come near to you.
JAMES 4:8

For God, who said, "Let light shine out of darkness," made his light shine in our hearts to give us the light of the knowledge of the glory of God in the face of Christ. But we have this treasure in jars of clay to show that this all-surpassing power is from God and not from us.
2 CORINTHIANS 4:6–7

WISDOM

ALL THE TREASURES OF WISDOM AND KNOWL-
EDGE ARE HIDDEN IN ME. So I am relevant to
absolutely everything! The world is such a fragmented
place, with many voices calling out to you—claiming to
have answers. When you are learning or experiencing
new things, it is vital to stay in communication with
Me. I can help you understand things from My perspective: drawing on My *magnificent wisdom*. I want you to
examine everything in the Light of biblical truth.

If you keep Me central in your thoughts, you can
discern order and design in a seemingly chaotic world.
There will continue to be things you cannot comprehend, because you live in a broken world and think
with a fallen, finite mind. So you must leave ample
room for *mystery* in your thinking. Acknowledging the
limits of your understanding opens the way to profound worship. You can exult in Me, the mysterious
Messiah who is infinite and good in every way. This
will encourage your heart as well as the hearts of your
fellow worshipers. To worship Me well, your hearts
must be *united in love*—woven into a beautiful Love-
tapestry. As you worship, thus united, you can enjoy
My majestic Presence *together* in ways that transcend

your individual experience. This enables you to venture further and further into My vast *hidden treasures of wisdom and knowledge.*

My purpose is that they may be encouraged in heart and united in love, so that they may have the full riches of complete understanding, in order that they may know the mystery of God, namely, Christ, in whom are hidden all the treasures of wisdom and knowledge.

COLOSSIANS 2:2–3

All this also comes from the LORD Almighty, wonderful in counsel and magnificent in wisdom.

ISAIAH 28:29

The fear of the LORD is the beginning of wisdom, and the knowledge of the Holy One is understanding.

PROVERBS 9:10 NKJV

HOPE

I AM YOUR RISEN, LIVING SAVIOR! Through My resurrection *you have been born again to an ever-living hope*. It is vital for you to remain hopeful, no matter what is going on in your life. People put their hope in a variety of things—wealth, power, health, medical treatments—but these are all insufficient. When storms break upon your life, you can find only one adequate source of help—Me! The hope I provide is *an anchor for your soul, firm and secure* even in the most tempestuous waters. A good way to remain anchored in Me is to whisper as often as needed: "Jesus, You are my Hope." This affirmation strengthens you and keeps you connected to Me.

I am constantly working to transform your life. You need My help continually to keep your hope alive. I stand ready to help you at *all* times—during stormy episodes as well as times of smooth sailing. I am not only *ever-living* but also more abundantly alive than you can possibly imagine. There are no limits to what My *great Power and Glory* can accomplish! I can change the most "hopeless" situation into outright victory. Moreover, as you affirm your trust in Me—no matter how difficult your circumstances—I am able to

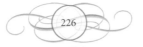

transform you: gradually, lovingly. *Those who hope in Me will not be disappointed.*

Praised (honored, blessed) be the God and Father of our Lord Jesus Christ(the Messiah)! By His boundless mercy we have been born again to an ever-living hope through the resurrection of Jesus Christ from the dead.

1 PETER 1:3 AMP

We have this hope as an anchor for the soul, firm and secure. It enters the inner sanctuary behind the curtain, where Jesus, who went before us, has entered on our behalf. He has become a high priest forever . . .

HEBREWS 6:19

Then they will see the Son of Man coming in the clouds with great power and glory.

MARK 13:26 NKJV

Then you will know that I am the LORD; those who hope in me will not be disappointed.

ISAIAH 49:23B

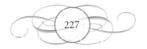

227

GRACE

I COMPREHEND YOU IN ALL YOUR COMPLEXITY; I UNDERSTAND YOU WITH ABSOLUTE ACCURACY; NO DETAIL OF YOUR LIFE IS HIDDEN FROM ME. Yet you need not be afraid of My intimate awareness, because I view you through eyes of grace.

Were I to look at you otherwise—through eyes of the law rather than eyes of grace—it could be terrifying to you. Unfortunately, you often view yourself that way: legalistically evaluating how well you're performing. When you think about it, you realize how silly that is, because your performance will never be sufficient to meet My holy standard.

Instead of focusing on your performance, come to Me and receive *My unfailing Love.* You are troubled by fear of failure, but My Love for you will never fail.

Here is what I see as I view you through eyes of grace: You look regal, for I have clothed you in My royal righteousness. You *are radiant*, especially when you are gazing at Me. You look lovely as you reflect My Glory back to Me. In fact, you delight Me so much that *I rejoice over you with shouts of Joy!*

Because I am infinite, I can see you simultaneously as you are now and as you will be in heaven. The

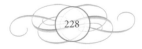

present view helps Me work with you on things you need to change. The heavenly vision enables Me to love you with perfect, everlasting Love.

The best way to see through eyes of grace is to gaze through the lens of *My unfailing Love*. As you persevere in this practice, you will gradually find it easier to extend grace both to yourself and to others.

How priceless is your unfailing love! Both high and low among men find refuge in the shadow of your wings.

PSALM 36:7

I sought the LORD, and he answered me; he delivered me from all my fears. Those who look to him are radiant; their faces are never covered with shame.

PSALM 34:4–5

The LORD your God is in your midst, a victorious warrior. He will exult over you with joy, He will be quiet in His love, He will rejoice over you with shouts of joy.

ZEPHANIAH 3:17 NASB

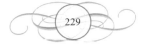

DEPENDING ON HIM

CLING TO ME AS YOUR LIFELINE. You need My help continually, and I am eager to provide it. Don't be anxious about your inability to *obey My voice* perfectly. The most important commandment is to *love Me with all your heart and with all your soul and with all your mind.* Although you can do this only imperfectly, I nonetheless delight in your love—as a mother delights in a crumpled flower brought lovingly by her child. Moreover, I rejoice in your obedience, though it is flawed, and in your desire to obey Me. Instead of worrying about the ways you fall short, focus on doing what you can—out of love for Me. Your awareness of your inadequacy can actually be a blessing: It protects you from self-righteousness. It also trains you to depend on Me more and more.

When you relate to Me as your Lifeline, I am pleased. Since *I am your Life,* looking to Me for help is the wisest way to live. I created you as a dependent being, and if you don't *cling to Me* you will grasp onto other things. This can lead to addictions, destructive relationships, and other forms of idolatry. So the more you hold onto Me, the better your life will be. I realize you are weak and your faith-muscles easily tire. When you feel as if you're about to lose your grip, cry out to

Me! *For I am the Lord, your God, who takes hold of your right hand and says to you, Do not fear; I will help you.*

"*That you may love the* LORD *your God, that you may obey His voice, and that you may cling to Him, for He is your life and the length of your days . . .*"
DEUTERONOMY 30:20 NKJV

Jesus replied: "'Love the Lord your God with all your heart and with all your soul and with all your mind.' This is the first and greatest commandment."
MATTHEW 22:37–38

For I am the LORD, *your God, who takes hold of your right hand and says to you, Do not fear; I will help you.*
ISAIAH 41:13

RIGHT LIVING

I URGE YOU TO USE WORDS WITH RESTRAINT. Misusing words is one of the easiest ways to sin—and one of the deadliest. In fact, *the tongue is a fire that corrupts the whole person, sets the whole course of his life on fire, and is itself set on fire by hell.* You would be wise to follow the example of David, who wrote: *Set a guard, O Lord, over my mouth; keep watch over the door of my lips.* Controlling your tongue is so difficult that you cannot do it without massive help.

Actually, I want to help you control not only your spoken words but also your thoughts. The contents of your thoughts have an enormous influence on your health and well-being. Many people are depressed or anxious because their thinking is so distorted and unbiblical. If this problem remains uncorrected, it can lead to a breakdown of health. However, Scripture provides correction: *Pleasant words are sweet to the soul and healing to the bones.* When My Spirit is controlling your thoughts and words, both your soul and your body will flourish. Ask the Spirit to think and speak through you. Since He lives in your innermost being He can easily influence you, but He waits to be invited. The more you invite Him into your life, the healthier

and happier you will be. Your words will be pleasant—
blessing not only you but also those around you.

*A man of knowledge uses words with restraint,
and a man of understanding is even-tempered.*
PROVERBS 17:27

*The tongue also is a fire, a world of evil among the parts
of the body. It corrupts the whole person, sets the whole
course of his life on fire, and is itself set on fire by hell.*
JAMES 3:6

*Set a guard, O LORD, over my mouth;
keep watch over the door of my lips.*
PSALM 141:3 NKJV

*Pleasant words are a honeycomb, sweet to
the soul and healing to the bones.*
PROVERBS 16:24

HIS LOVE

Long before you began seeking Me, I had designs on you for glorious living. My *overall purpose* embraces and enfolds you—helping you understand who you are, giving meaning to your life. *In Me you live and move and have your being.* Even before the earth's creation I chose you *as the focus of My Love, to be made whole and holy by My Love.* Until you came to know Me as Savior, your life was painfully incomplete. Your inner being was rife with gaping holes. Only My limitless Love is sufficient to fill all that emptiness! The healing and wholeness you are finding in Me will continue to increase as you mature in My ways.

My Love not only completes you; it also makes you holy. Your awareness that I love you with perfect, unending Love helps you break free from sinful ways. Growth in holiness is a process, of course, and sometimes it is painful. But the pleasures of My boundless Love outweigh any amount of pain and trouble you experience. When you are suffering, talk with Me about your struggles. *Pour out your heart to Me.* As I soothe you with My loving Presence, I reassure you of *the overall purpose I am working out in everything and everyone*—in you!

It's in Christ that we find out who we are and what we are living for. Long before we first heard of Christ and got our hopes up, he had his eye on us, had designs on us for glorious living, part of the overall purpose he is working out in everything and everyone.

<small>EPHESIANS 1:11–12 MSG</small>

"For in him we live and move and have our being." As some of your own poets have said, "We are his offspring."

<small>ACTS 17:28</small>

Long before he laid down earth's foundations, he had us in mind, had settled on us as the focus of his love, to be made whole and holy by his love.

<small>EPHESIANS 1:4 MSG</small>

Trust in him at all times, O people; pour out your hearts to him, for God is our refuge.

<small>PSALM 62:8</small>

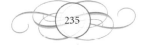

HEAVEN

BE CONTENT TO BE ONE OF MY SHEEP—
ETERNALLY KNOWN, ETERNALLY SECURE. I
want you to *hear My voice*, so you can *follow Me* closely
all the days and moments of your life. I speak to you
in many ways, though most clearly through My Word.
You need to maintain a listening attitude in order to
hear Me. This requires both patience and perseverance: waiting in My Presence, eager to hear from Me.
I, your Shepherd-King, not only lead you through each
day of your life; I also open to you the gates of heaven.
You do well to remember that the Shepherd who so
tenderly leads you is the King of eternity.

Though your earth-body will someday die, you
yourself *will never perish*. When you become *absent
from the body*, you will *be present with Me* in a deep,
rich, glorious way beyond anything you can imagine!
No one will be able to *snatch you out of My hand*. This
assurance of your eternal destiny sets you free from
fear of death. It also strengthens you to live bountifully
today—joyously following your Shepherd.

Sheep are not designed to live independently.
They need a wise, loving shepherd to guide them
carefully. Similarly, you live best when you follow Me

humbly, in sheep-like fashion. As you trust Me to know what is best for you, I lovingly *guide you in paths of righteousness.*

"My sheep hear My voice, and I know them,
and they follow Me. And I give them eternal life,
and they shall never perish; neither shall
anyone snatch them out of My hand."
JOHN 10:27–28 NKJV

*We are confident, yes, well pleased rather to be absent
from the body and to be present with the Lord.*
2 CORINTHIANS 5:8 NKJV

*The LORD is my shepherd, I shall not be in want.
He makes me lie down in green pastures, he leads me
beside quiet waters, he restores my soul. He guides me
in paths of righteousness for his name's sake.*
PSALM 23:1–3

PEACE

I AM YOUR SUNRISE FROM ON HIGH! While you were still *sitting in darkness and the shadow of death,* My Light shone upon you—giving you a reason to live, a reason to hope. Now you are Mine, and you can approach Me confidently because of My *tender mercy.* My heart is full of *unfailing Love* for you; it overflows from My heart into yours. As you receive good things from Me with thanksgiving, you experience rich soul-satisfaction. I want you to *sing for Joy and be glad* in response to all that I give you. You can relax and enjoy My Presence since you know I am taking care of you. *In your time of need,* I will provide *mercy and grace to help you.*

I want you to enjoy not only My Presence but also My Peace. I came into your world *to guide your feet into the way of Peace.* When you are anxious or fearful, it is as if you are doubting My promises to *supply all you need.* My followers tend to think of worry as natural, even inevitable. At worst, they consider it their personal problem or quirk—harming no one but themselves. But the truth is, your tendency to be anxious grieves Me. Awareness of My pain can help motivate you to break free from this hurtful habit. Seek to bring Me Joy by walking trustingly with Me along the path of Peace.

*Because of the tender mercy of our God, with which
the Sunrise from on high shall visit us, to shine upon
those who sit in darkness and the shadow of death,
to guide our feet into the way of peace.*
LUKE 1:78–79 NASB

*Satisfy us in the morning with your unfailing love,
that we may sing for joy and be glad all our days.*
PSALM 90:14

*Let us then approach the throne of grace with
confidence, so that we may receive mercy and
find grace to help us in our time of need.*
HEBREWS 4:16

*And my God will supply all your needs according
to His riches in glory in Christ Jesus.*
PHILIPPIANS 4:19 NASB

PLEASING HIM

SEEK TO PLEASE ME ABOVE ALL ELSE. Let this be your guiding focus throughout the day so that you won't be sidetracked by lesser goals.

You will not be able to achieve success through discipline alone, for this pursuit requires more than your willpower: It is mainly powered by what is in your heart. As your Love for Me grows stronger, so does your desire to please Me. When a man and a woman are deeply in love, they take great delight in pleasing one another. They may spend hours pondering ways to surprise their beloved with unexpected pleasures. Simply anticipating the loved one's happiness is exciting to such a lover. I Myself am such a Lover! I delight in increasing your Joy: making it complete. The best way to grow in your passion for Me is to increase your awareness of My ardent Love for you.

Whenever you seek to please Me, think about Me as the Lover of your soul: the One who loves you perfectly every nanosecond of your existence. Let your budding desire to please Me flourish in the Light of *My unfailing Love.*

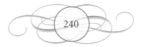

And we pray this in order that you may live a life
worthy of the Lord and may please him in every way:
bearing fruit in every good work, growing in the
knowledge of God . . .

COLOSSIANS 1:10

Therefore, holy brothers, who share in the heavenly
calling, fix your thoughts on Jesus, the apostle
and high priest whom we confess.

HEBREWS 3:1

As the Father has loved me, so have I loved you.
Now remain in my love. If you obey my commands,
you will remain in my love, just as I have obeyed my
Father's commands and remain in his love. I have
told you this so that my joy may be in you and
that your joy may be complete.

JOHN 15:9–11

But I am like an olive tree flourishing in the house of
God; I trust in God's unfailing love for ever and ever.

PSALM 52:8

RESTING IN HIM

THOUGH YOU SIT IN DARKNESS I WILL BE YOUR LIGHT. Sometimes you need to rest in the shadows. If you continue pushing yourself—ignoring how weary you are—you may collapse altogether. Many of My followers drive themselves to the point of exhaustion or utter discouragement, while pretending everything is all right. *Your enemy the devil* rejoices—even gloats—when he sees this happening. He understands the power of pretense to weaken My children till they are easy prey for him.

Do not panic when *you have fallen*, for *you will rise* again. Be content to *sit in darkness* while I refresh your spirit, mind, and body. I am as fully present with you when you are sitting as when you are standing or walking. Look for Me in the shadowy place where you find yourself now. I want to shelter and nurture you *under My wings*, where *you will find refuge*. While you are relaxing, *I will be your Light*—protecting, healing, and restoring you.

When My work of restoration is finished, you can crawl out from under My wings: ready to rise again and continue your journey. My Presence will go with you, illuminating the way before you—strengthening

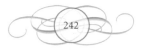

and encouraging you. *Hope in Me, My child, for you will again praise Me for the help of My Presence.*

> *Do not gloat over me, my enemy!*
> *Though I have fallen, I will rise. Though I sit*
> *in darkness the LORD will be my light.*
> MICAH 7:8

> *Be self-controlled and alert. Your enemy*
> *the devil prowls around like a roaring lion*
> *looking for someone to devour.*
> 1 PETER 5:8

> *He will cover you with his feathers, and under*
> *his wings you will find refuge; his faithfulness*
> *will be your shield and rampart.*
> PSALM 91:4

> *Why are you in despair, O my soul? And why have you*
> *become disturbed within me? Hope in God, for I shall*
> *again praise Him for the help of His presence.*
> PSALM 42:5 NASB

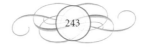

243

INTIMACY WITH HIM

I AM IMMANUEL—GOD WITH YOU. Your pursuit of Me is actually a response to My ardent pursuit of you. You don't have to batter down doors between us. Rather, as you open the door of your heart to Me, you find Me gloriously present—*having already thrown open My door to you!*

My death on the cross for your sins was sufficient to open up My door to you permanently. Ever since you trusted Me as Savior, your standing with Me has been eternally secure. So you need not fear that on a day when your performance is below par I might shut the door in your face. With My help you can break out of that narrow enclosure of performance anxiety. I designed you to flourish in *the wide open spaces of My grace and glory*, where you are free to celebrate My Presence exuberantly. *Stand tall and shout praises* to Me, remembering you are royalty in My kingdom of never-ending Life.

I want you to realize how utterly safe you are—in My perfect, persistent Love. You understand that the strength of *your* love is insufficient to keep you connected with Me. You know you cannot rely on your own faithfulness. That's why you must depend on My unfailing provision. *Love and faithfulness meet together in Me; moreover, through the sacrifice of My blood, righteousness and peace kiss each other.*

"Behold, the virgin shall be with child, and bear
a Son, and they shall call His name Immanuel,"
which is translated, "God with us."
MATTHEW 1:23 NKJV

We throw open our doors to God and discover at the
same moment that he has already thrown open his door
to us. We find ourselves standing where we always hoped
we might stand—out in the wide open spaces of God's
grace and glory, standing tall and shouting our praise.
ROMANS 5:2 MSG

He brought me out into a spacious place; he
rescued me because he delighted in me.
PSALM 18:19

Love and faithfulness meet together;
righteousness and peace kiss each other.
PSALM 85:10

245

JOY

REJOICE IN THIS DAY OF LIFE, BEING WILLING TO FOLLOW ME WHOLEHEARTEDLY—WHER-EVER I LEAD. Anticipate blessings as we journey together. Since I have created this day of life and pre-sented it to you free of charge, I want you to receive it gratefully. Your natural tendency when you awaken is to assess the day before you, trying to discern how good (or bad) it will be. You do this almost unconsciously, often basing your conclusions on something as trivial as the weather. I urge you to break free from this habit so you can be more receptive to Me and My blessings.

A thankful attitude is immensely helpful. If you awaken to find a dark, rainy day, you can thank Me for the rain. Having done so, you will be much less likely to grumble about the weather. Also, remember that *I* have arranged the conditions of your day. So you can assume there is much good to be found in it.

Rejoicing will help you find many blessings in this day. If your circumstances are looking rather bleak, then be joyful in Me—your faithful Companion. I want you to enjoy Me and look for precious gifts I've placed along the path we are following. In faith, be on the lookout for good things both great and small. Also,

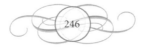

because I am your *Teacher*, I promise to provide learning opportunities as we travel together.

When you reach the end of this day, stop and look back at the distance we have covered. Take time to ponder what you have learned and to savor the gifts you have found. Let your mind dwell on these things as you *lie down to sleep*, rejoicing in Me and My blessings.

This is the day the LORD has made;
let us rejoice and be glad in it.
PSALM 118:24

"You call me 'Teacher' and 'Lord,' and
rightly so, for that is what I am."
JOHN 13:13

I lie down and sleep; I wake again,
because the LORD sustains me.
PSALM 3:5

CONTROL

I AM YOUR INTIMATE FRIEND, BUT I AM ALSO UNFATHOMABLE AND MYSTERIOUS; INFINITELY GREAT AND GLORIOUS! I want you to contemplate Me in My Glory so you can worship Me exuberantly. Sometimes, though, you struggle with My *unsearchable decisions and untraceable ways*—seeking to control Me rather than abandoning yourself to Me in worship. You need to recognize "control" for what it is: an idol. I created you in My image and endowed you with free will. I gave you amazing linguistic abilities so you could communicate richly with Me. Instead of using these gifts in manipulative ways—trying to control Me—devote them to worshiping Me *in spirit and truth*.

I encourage you to pray freely: *Ask and it will be given to you.* Nonetheless, when you bring Me your petitions, you need to keep in mind the *depth of My wisdom and knowledge.* This will protect you from being presumptuous or manipulative. I never fail to hear your prayers and answer them wisely, but I do not always grant your petitions—no matter how heartfelt they may be and how utterly right they may seem. If it becomes clear that My will differs from what you have requested, the best response is to say simply, "Yes, Jesus."

This will draw you closer to Me, even in the midst of your disappointment. Though My ways—*My methods, My paths*—may be mysterious from your perspective, I assure you they are good.

Oh, the depth of the riches and wisdom and knowledge of God! How unfathomable (inscrutable, unsearchable) are His judgments (His decisions)! And how untraceable (mysterious, undiscoverable) are His ways (His methods, His paths)!
ROMANS 11:33 AMP

God is Spirit, and those who worship Him must worship in spirit and truth.
JOHN 4:24 NKJV

Ask and it will be given to you; seek and you will find; knock and the door will be opened to you.
MATTHEW 7:7

TRUST

REST IN THE ASSURANCE OF MY SHELTERING PRESENCE THAT KEEPS YOU SAFE. Let My promises of protection strengthen and comfort you—like huge heavenly bells pealing out ancient, changeless truth. I want you to take refuge in My *Shaddai-shadow* more and more, by placing your trust fully in Me. It is tempting to take shelter in people, money, success, good health. These are blessings from Me, but you must not rely on them. Any or all of them could vanish instantly. The unending protection I offer—*refuge in the shadow of My wings*—is available to *both high and low among men*. In addition, I freely give you the priceless gift of *My unfailing Love!*

Since I offer you so much, it makes sense to put your trust in Me above all else. Listen to the psalmist's proclamation: *It is better to take refuge in the Lord than to trust in man. It is better to take refuge in the Lord than to trust in princes.* Solomon, the wisest of all men, wrote: *He who trusts in his riches will fall.* Whenever you start to feel anxious, let these feelings serve as a warning that you're putting your trust in the wrong place. You need to stop listening to your worry-thoughts, and instead tell yourself the truth—that I am *totally* trustworthy.

Then turn your attention to Me, saying: *"Lord, You're my refuge. I trust in You and I'm safe!"*

You who sit down in the High God's presence, spend the night in Shaddai's shadow, say this: "GOD, you're my refuge. I trust in you and I'm safe!"
PSALM 91:1–2 MSG

How priceless is your unfailing love! Both high and low among men find refuge in the shadow of your wings.
PSALM 36:7

It is better to take refuge in the LORD than to trust in man. It is better to take refuge in the LORD than to trust in princes.
PSALM 118:8–9

He who trusts in his riches will fall, but the righteous will flourish like foliage.
PROVERBS 11:28 NKJV

ABIDING IN HIM

YOU LIVE BY THE SPIRIT: HE IS THE VERY SOURCE OF YOUR ETERNAL LIFE. When *you were dead in trespasses and sins*, it was impossible for you to receive Me as Savior. The Holy Spirit had to *make you alive* before you could respond to Me. So you do quite literally *live by the Spirit*.

I want you to go forward along your life-path *in step with the Spirit*. He will not help you go backward, so beware of seeking refuge in the past. You need to keep moving forward and also to walk in the direction I choose. Moreover, it's vital to pace yourself according to My timing: neither dashing ahead nor lagging behind. The Spirit will help you in all these matters, as you live in reliance on Him. You can engage His help any time, any place—simply by asking. If you find yourself anxiously rushing, pray "Slow me down, Holy Spirit." If you're uncertain about your direction, ask Him to show you the way. When you *don't know how to pray as you should*, cry out "Help me, Holy Spirit!" He will *intercede for you with groanings too deep for words*.

The more you seek My Spirit's help and yield to His loving guidance, the better your life will be. As you *keep in step with the Spirit*, you find yourself walking close to Me.

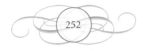

Since we live by the Spirit,
let us keep in step with the Spirit.
GALATIANS 5:25

And you He made alive, who were dead in
trespasses and sins, in which you once walked
according to the course of this world . . .
EPHESIANS 2:1–2 NKJV

Show me your ways, O LORD, teach me your paths;
guide me in your truth and teach me, for you are God
my Savior, and my hope is in you all day long.
PSALM 25:4–5

In the same way the Spirit also helps our weakness;
for we do not know how to pray as we should,
but the Spirit Himself intercedes for us
with groanings too deep for words.
ROMANS 8:26 NASB

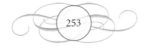

CONDEMNATION

I AM THE PERFECT SAVIOR—100 PERCENT GOD AND 100 PERCENT MAN. I came to earth in a *physical body* so I could bear all the punishment for your sins. Because you are Mine, you are indeed *holy in My sight, without blemish and free from accusation*. I know you sometimes *feel* blemished and accused, but this is not your true identity. Now that you're My redeemed follower, a good word to describe you is "blameless." Since I paid the penalty *through death* for all your sins, you are utterly free from blame. There is *no condemnation* for those who are united with Me through faith!

Although you are forever *free from accusation*, you have a persistent adversary. Satan is a relentless accuser of Christians; he *accuses them day and night*. His demonic underlings, who seek to deceive and destroy My followers, rely heavily on this tactic. These evil spirits attack your mind with a mixture of lies and truth. To counteract their attacks, try writing down the accusing thoughts so you can pick out the distortions and outright lies. Once you have done this, the most effective response is straightforward: Reject the lies and distortions; repent of any actual sin. Remember, though, that the bottom line is not what you do but what I have *already* done—redeemed you fully so you can live with Me eternally. When *the Son makes you free*, you are *free indeed!*

But now he has reconciled you by Christ's physical body through death to present you holy in His sight, without blemish and free from accusation.

COLOSSIANS 1:22

Therefore there is now no condemnation for those who are in Christ Jesus.

ROMANS 8:1 NASB

Then I heard a loud voice in heaven say: "Now have come the salvation and the power and the kingdom of our God, and the authority of his Christ. For the accuser of our brothers, who accuses them before our God day and night, has been hurled down.

REVELATION 12:10

Therefore if the Son makes you free, you shall be free indeed.

JOHN 8:36 NKJV

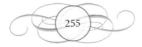

255

HIS PRESENCE

I AM NEARER THAN YOU DARE BELIEVE, CLOSER THAN THE AIR YOU BREATHE. Usually, you're not conscious of being enveloped in air because it is invisible and constantly available to you. Similarly, My unseen Presence is a constant in your life, but you often fail to recognize Me. This leaves you vulnerable to loneliness. If you could always recognize My Presence, you would never feel lonely again.

I deeply desire for you to experience My nearness—and the peaceful contentment it brings—more consistently. There is a close connection between feeling lonely and being unaware of My Presence. This is an age-old problem: When the patriarch Jacob was in a barren place—far from his family—he was quite conscious of his isolation. However, I poured out My Presence upon him in the form of a glorious dream. When Jacob awoke, he responded, *"Surely the LORD is in this place, and I was not aware of it."*

Awareness of My abiding Presence will protect you from loneliness. Not only am I constantly with you, but I am also within you: in the inner recesses of your heart and mind. My knowledge of you is picture-perfect, and it is framed in unconditional Love.

Let feelings of loneliness remind you of your need to seek My Face. Come to Me with your ever-so-human emptiness, and My divine Presence will fill you with *Life to the full!*

In my integrity you uphold me and set me
in your presence forever.
PSALM 41:12

When Jacob awoke from his sleep, he thought, "Surely
the LORD is in this place, and I was not aware of it."
GENESIS 28:16

O LORD, you have searched me and you know me.
You know when I sit and when I rise;
you perceive my thoughts from afar.
PSALM 139:1–2

The thief comes only to steal and kill and destroy; I have
come that they may have life, and have it to the full.
JOHN 10:10

HEAVEN

LIFT UP YOUR EYES TO ME, AND SEE ME SHINING BRIGHTLY ON YOUR FUTURE. Your body—especially when it is weak and weary—can exert a strong downward pull on your thinking. This is very natural, but you are not limited to natural abilities. When your thoughts are on a downhill path, you need to access supernatural resources. Ask Me to help you think *My* thoughts. Refuse to entertain a gloomy view of the future. Reject such imagery as unreal, because that is what it is. Any future-view that does not include Me is simply false! I am the most important ingredient in the mix of your life. The more of Me you include, the better your outlook will be.

Do not be overly focused on the condition of your body, since it is temporary. Instead, rejoice that your inner being—the eternal part of you—is *being renewed day by day.* You can even glean some good from the progressive *wasting away* of your outer self. As your natural strengths and abilities wane, you become more aware of your need to rely on Me. This can create a relaxed intimacy between us as you include Me in more and more of your moments. Not only does this increase your Joy in the present, it also prepares you for an eternal future face to Face with Me.

This is the true view of your future, and it is glorious! So, *fix your eyes not on what is seen, but on what is unseen. For what is seen is temporary, but what is unseen is eternal.*

I will lift up my eyes to the hills—from whence comes my help? My help comes from the LORD, who made heaven and earth.

PSALM 121:1–2 NKJV

We demolish arguments and every pretension that sets itself up against the knowledge of God, and we take captive every thought to make it obedient to Christ.

2 CORINTHIANS 10:5

Therefore we do not lose heart. Though outwardly we are wasting away, yet inwardly we are being renewed day by day. For our light and momentary troubles are achieving for us an eternal glory that far outweighs them all. So we fix our eyes not on what is seen, but on what is unseen. For what is seen is temporary, but what is unseen is eternal.

2 CORINTHIANS 4:16–18

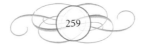

HIS FAITHFULNESS

MY COMPASSIONS NEVER FAIL; THEY ARE NEW EVERY MORNING. You can begin each day confidently, knowing that My vast reservoir of blessings is full—to the brim. This knowledge helps you *wait for Me*, entrusting your long-unanswered prayers into My care and keeping. I assure you that not one of your prayers has slipped past Me, unnoticed. I want you to drink deeply from My fountain of limitless Love and unfailing compassion. As you wait in My Presence, these divine nutrients are freely available. You may *drink without cost from the spring of the water of Life.*

Although many of your prayers remain unanswered, you can trust in *My great faithfulness:* I keep all My promises in My perfect way and timing. Among other things, I have promised to *give you Peace* that displaces the trouble and fear in your heart.

If you become weary of waiting for answers to your prayers, remember that I also wait: so that *I may be gracious to you* and *have mercy on you.* I wait till you are ready to receive the things I have lovingly prepared for you. *Blessed are all those who wait for Me*—expectantly, longingly, trustingly.

*Because of the LORD's great love we are not consumed,
for his compassions never fail. They are new every
morning; great is your faithfulness. I say to myself,
"The LORD is my portion; therefore I will wait for him."*

LAMENTATIONS 3:22–24

*He said to me: "It is done. I am the Alpha
and the Omega, the Beginning and the End.
To him who is thirsty I will give to drink without
cost from the spring of the water of life."*

REVELATION 21:6

*"Peace I leave with you; my peace I give you. I do not
give to you as the world gives. Do not let your
hearts be troubled and do not be afraid."*

JOHN 14:27

*Therefore the LORD will wait, that He may be
gracious to you; and . . . that He may have mercy
on you. For the LORD is a God of justice; blessed
are all those who wait for Him.*

ISAIAH 30:18 NKJV

PROTECTION

DO NOT FEAR, FOR I—YOUR GOD—AM WITH YOU. *I will uphold you with My righteous right hand.* Let these words enfold you like a warm blanket, sheltering you from the coldness of fear and dismay. When trouble seems to be stalking you, grip My hand tightly and stay in communication with Me. You can *trust and not be afraid,* for I am your *Strength and Song.* My powerful Presence is with you at all times; you face *nothing* alone. Moreover, I have promised to *strengthen you and help you.* Awareness of these truths can fill you with Joy and Peace.

My righteous right hand holds you up in both good times and bad. When things are flowing smoothly in your life, you may be unaware of My sustaining Presence. Should I cease to support you, though, you would quickly fall. When you are *walking through the valley of the shadow of death*—keenly aware of your neediness—you gratefully cling to My strong hand. *My right hand sustains you* during these times of affliction, enabling you to keep putting one foot in front of the other. As you endure your trials in trusting dependence on Me, I bless you in the midst of hardship. I even *stoop down to make you great:* I reach down—into

the valley of affliction—and lift you up into sacred
pleasures shared with Me.

So do not fear, for I am with you; do not be dismayed,
for I am your God. I will strengthen you and help you;
I will uphold you with my righteous right hand.
ISAIAH 41:10

"Behold, God is my salvation, I will trust and not be
afraid; for the LORD GOD is my strength and song,
and He has become my salvation."
ISAIAH 12:2 NASB

Yea, though I walk through the valley of the
shadow of death, I will fear no evil; for You are with me;
Your rod and Your staff, they comfort me.
PSALM 23:4 NKJV

You give me your shield of victory, and your right hand
sustains me; you stoop down to make me great.
PSALM 18:35

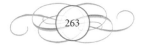

263

FREEDOM IN HIM

I APPROACH YOU WITH TENDERNESS, BECAUSE YOU ARE PRECIOUS TO ME AND I KNOW HOW FRAGILE YOU ARE. *I draw you with gentle cords, with bands of Love.* These Love-cords keep you connected to Me; they also help you discern *the way you should go.* Though My bands of Love are unbreakable, they do not curtail your freedom. These highly elastic bands allow you to go your own way for a while. However, even if they are stretched out for a long time—as you seek to live independently of Me—they retain their drawing power. Eventually, when you grow weary of worldly ways, the cords draw you gently back to Me. No matter how far you have roamed, I welcome you with *unfailing Love.*

I stoop down both to nourish you and to liberate you: *take the yoke from your neck.* The yoke is a symbol of slavery, and you have been *a slave to sin.* My death on the cross for your sins provided a way to free you from this slavery. *I have broken the bands of your yoke* and replaced them with *bands of Love.* Now you can *walk upright*—with your head held high—rejoicing in Me, your Savior. *When the Son sets you free, you are free indeed!*

I drew them with gentle cords, with bands of love,
and I was to them as those who take the yoke from
their neck. I stooped and fed them.
HOSEA 11:4 NKJV

Let the morning bring me word of your unfailing love,
for I have put my trust in you. Show me the way I
should go, for to you I lift up my soul.
PSALM 143:8

Jesus replied, "I tell you the truth, everyone who
sins is a slave to sin. Now a slave has no permanent
place in the family, but a son belongs to it forever. So if
the Son sets you free, you will be free indeed."
JOHN 8:34–36

"I am the LORD your God, who brought you
out of the land of Egypt, that you should not be
their slaves; I have broken the bands of your
yoke and made you walk upright."
LEVITICUS 26:13 NKJV

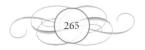

265

RESTING IN HIM

COME TO ME JUST AS YOU ARE. Let Me enfold you in My compassionate embrace. I know the depth and breadth of your weariness. I see you from the inside out, as well as from the outside in. Nothing about you escapes My attention—or My tender concern. I offer you rest, My child, but in order to receive it you must stop for a time and simply wait with Me. When you are physically tired, your mind easily succumbs to anxious thoughts. Then, although your body needs rest, the anxiety drives you harder than ever. This is hurtful and counterproductive.

Discipline yourself to stop whatever you are doing, and take time to *fix your thoughts on Me*. I provide rest not only for your mind and body but also *for your soul*. However, your body and soul cannot rest until your mind settles down. Take quiet, slow breaths while you focus your attention on Me. It can be helpful to say a simple prayer such as: "Jesus, fill me with Your Peace." Since My Peace *surpasses all understanding*, your mind will eventually relax in My Presence. You can unburden yourself by *making your requests known to Me*. This transfers your burdens to My strong shoulders. Remember to bring Me your requests *with thanksgiving*, for I delight

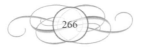

in responding to thankful prayers. Moreover, your grateful attitude will bless you immeasurably—opening wide your heart to receive more and more of Me.

"Come to me, all you who are weary and burdened, and I will give you rest. Take my yoke upon you and learn from me, for I am gentle and humble in heart, and you will find rest for your souls."

MATTHEW 11:28–29

Therefore, holy brothers, who share in the heavenly calling, fix your thoughts on Jesus, the apostle and high priest whom we confess.

HEBREWS 3:1

Be anxious for nothing, but in everything by prayer and supplication, with thanksgiving, let your requests be made known to God; and the peace of God, which surpasses all understanding, will guard your hearts and minds through Christ Jesus.

PHILIPPIANS 4:6–7 NKJV

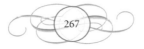

WISDOM

REAL, ETERNAL WISDOM IS ALL ABOUT KNOW-
ING ME. There is not only wisdom but also great
pleasure to be found in heart-knowledge of Me. This
pleasure far surpasses anything the world has to offer.
Moreover, *those who are wise will shine like the brightness of the heavens.* So you will be wonderfully rewarded
for your wise practice of enjoying My Presence—an
incredible privilege in itself. The perceptive ones in My
kingdom are those who have true understanding of Me
that is grounded in My Word. The more you absorb
Scripture—allowing it to penetrate your heart, mind,
and spirit—the better you can know Me. *All* those who
know Me as Savior will shine in heaven forever. Let this
sparkling promise fill you with bright hope.

Another awesome privilege I offer you is to *lead
many to righteousness.* Your life and your words can influence others for righteousness in various ways: *If anyone
among you wanders from the truth,* I can use you to help
that straying one *turn from the error of his way.* Also, as
you seek to live near Me, enjoying My Presence, *your light
shines before men*—helping them find Me. Influencing
others for righteousness increases your ability to *shine
like the stars for ever and ever.* Thus, living close to Me

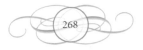

not only blesses you now but also enlarges your capacity to reflect My Glory through all eternity!

Those who are wise will shine like the brightness of the heavens, and those who lead many to righteousness, like the stars for ever and ever.

DANIEL 12:3

Your word is a lamp to my feet and a light for my path.

PSALM 119:105

Brethren, if anyone among you wanders from the truth, and someone turns him back, let him know that he who turns a sinner from the error of his way will save a soul from death and cover a multitude of sins.

JAMES 5:19–20 NKJV

In the same way, let your light shine before men, that they may see your good deeds and praise your Father in heaven.

MATTHEW 5:16

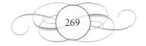

TRANSFORMATION

YOU ARE A CHILD OF GOD, AND YOU ARE MINE FOREVER. Someday you will *see Me as I am*—face to Face in Glory. You have been a member of My royal family since the moment you trusted Me as Savior. I am training you in the ways of My kingdom: *to be made new in the attitude of your mind; to put on the new self, created to be like Me.* Although your new self is being conformed to My image, this process does not erase the essence of who you are. On the contrary, the more you become *like Me*, the more you develop into the unique person I designed you to be.

Since you are part of My royal family, you're a *fellow heir with Me*—sharing My inheritance. However, *you must share My suffering if you are to share My Glory.* You don't need to search for ways to suffer. Living in this broken world provides ample opportunity to experience pain of many kinds. When adversity comes your way, search for Me in the midst of your struggles. Ask Me to help you suffer well, in a manner worthy of royalty. Everything you endure can help you become more like Me. Remember the ultimate goal: *You will see My Face in righteousness*—and *be satisfied!*

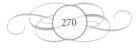

*Beloved, now we are children of God; and it
has not yet been revealed what we shall be, but we
know that when He is revealed, we shall be
like Him, for we shall see Him as He is.*

1 JOHN 3:2 NKJV

*You were taught, with regard to your former way of
life, to put off your old self, . . . to be made new in the
attitude of your minds; and to put on the new self,
created to be like God in true righteousness and holiness.*

EPHESIANS 4:22–24

*And if we are [His] children, then we are [His] heirs
also: heirs of God and fellow heirs with Christ [sharing
His inheritance with Him]; only we must share His
suffering if we are to share His glory.*

ROMANS 8:17 AMP

*As for me, I will see Your face in righteousness; I shall
be satisfied when I awake in Your likeness.*

PSALM 17:15 NKJV

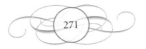

WORRY

THE ULTIMATE PROTECTION AGAINST SINKING DURING LIFE'S STORMS IS DEVELOPING YOUR FRIENDSHIP WITH ME. You waste a lot of time, however, worrying about storms you can see forming along the horizon of your life. In the past many of the storms you had anticipated veered off in another direction, never reaching you. Although some of them did actually hit, usually they had lost much of their power by the time they got to you. I urge you to switch your focus from difficulties that *may* come your way to My Presence, which is *always* with you.

You will never find security by trying to anticipate all the storms that may reach you someday. Remember that I control the atmosphere of your life. Trust Me by relaxing and releasing your concerns into My capable care. It saddens Me to see you obsessing about possible problems rather than bringing these matters to Me. When you find yourself anxiously scanning the horizon of your life, use that as a reminder to *seek My Face*. You will not find Me off in the distance. I am here beside you, nearer than you dare believe.

Instead of wasting time worrying, devote that time to building close friendship with Me. Talk with Me

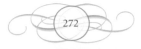

about everything that concerns you—your pleasures as well as your problems. I am interested in everything that matters to you because I am your perpetual Lover. Remember that *I am holding you by your right hand. I guide you with My own counsel*, based on eternal wisdom; so there's no need to worry about the future. When the time comes, I will personally *take you into Glory*. For now just live *near Me*. My friendship is your best refuge in the storms of life.

Look to the LORD and his strength; seek his face always.
1 CHRONICLES 16:11

I have loved you with an everlasting love;
I have drawn you with loving-kindness.
JEREMIAH 31:3

Yet I am always with you; you hold me by my right hand. You guide me with your counsel, and afterward you will take me into glory. . . . But as for me, it is good to be near God. I have made the Sovereign LORD my refuge; I will tell of all your deeds.
PSALM 73:23–24, 28

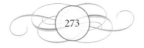

273

GRACE

Your relationship with Me is saturated in grace. Therefore, nothing you do or don't do can separate you from My Presence. When you are keenly aware of having failed Me, feelings of guilt and fear will conspire to convince you that you have lost My Love. Your sense of unworthiness will tempt you to punish yourself for your sins. But remember: *I have clothed you with garments of salvation—arrayed you in My own righteousness*. Your salvation is all about Me and what I have done to rescue you. Let me help you feel more secure in My Love.

At times of deep regret, you need to grasp onto grace for dear life. It is utterly impossible for Me to stop loving you. Your relationship with Me is so saturated in grace that the two are forever inseparable. Consider the following: Meat that has been marinated cannot become unmarinated. The longer it soaks, the deeper the marinade penetrates, flavoring and tenderizing the meat. You have been soaking in grace ever since you trusted Me as Savior. The longer you "marinate," the more fully My grace permeates our relationship. It is impossible for you to become un-graced!

I want you to rest in the perfection of your salvation. *My glorious grace* makes you *holy and blameless*

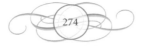

in My sight. So, nothing you do or fail to do could ever separate you from My Love.

For by grace you have been saved through faith, and that not of yourselves; it is the gift of God, not of works, lest anyone should boast.
EPHESIANS 2:8–9 NKJV

I delight greatly in the LORD; my soul rejoices in my God. For he has clothed me with garments of salvation and arrayed me in a robe of righteousness . . .
ISAIAH 61:10

For he chose us in him before the creation of the world to be holy and blameless in his sight. In love he predestined us to be adopted as his sons through Jesus Christ, in accordance with his pleasure and will—to the praise of his glorious grace, which he has freely given us in the One he loves.
EPHESIANS 1:4–6

Neither height nor depth, nor anything else in all creation, will be able to separate us from the love of God that is in Christ Jesus our Lord.
ROMANS 8:39

BROKENNESS

I AM THE HIGH AND EXALTED ONE WHOSE NAME IS HOLY. Yet I choose to dwell with people who are contrite and lowly of spirit. I know how prone to pride My people are, so I provide a variety of circumstances to humble them. You don't need to look for ways to become more humble. If you try with all your might to be *lowly of spirit*, you are more likely to become proud—or even ridiculous. Instead, you need to be on the lookout for what *I* am doing in your life and yield yourself to My ways. Your focus should not be on how humble you are but on how you can please Me in the present moment.

Being contrite—repentant for your sins—is another matter altogether. You *do* need to examine yourself and become aware of your sins, so you can confess them to Me and enjoy the freedom of forgiveness. Ask the Holy Spirit to help you see what is truly sinful, while protecting you from the trap of false guilt. As you face your flaws, open your heart to My loving Presence. I am *near to those who have a broken heart and a contrite spirit*. Moreover, I *revive the spirit of the lowly and the heart of the contrite*. So this way of humility and repentance is actually a path of intimacy with Me—leading to bountiful Joy. As you walk trustingly along this path with Me, *My unfailing Love surrounds you.*

For thus says the high and exalted One who lives forever, whose name is Holy, "I dwell on a high and holy place, and also with the contrite and lowly of spirit in order to revive the spirit of the lowly and to revive the heart of the contrite."

ISAIAH 57:15 NASB

Humble yourselves, therefore, under God's mighty hand, that he may lift you up in due time.

1 PETER 5:6

The LORD is near to those who have a broken heart, and saves such as have a contrite spirit.

PSALM 34:18 NKJV

Many are the woes of the wicked, but the LORD's unfailing love surrounds the man who trusts in him.

PSALM 32:10

277

HIS LOVE

I TAKE GREAT DELIGHT IN YOU, I REJOICE OVER
YOU WITH SINGING. Sometimes you feel unworthy of this amazing Love. No one could ever be good
enough or work hard enough to *deserve* My Love, but
I have chosen to relate to you *mercifully*. My death on
the cross completely satisfied justice, opening the way
for Me to show you mercy. As your resurrected Savior,
I am free to bestow eternal Life and Love on all who
believe in Me. I *beautify the humble with salvation*, and
I unashamedly *take pleasure in My people*.

I love you passionately, but I don't want you to
feel overwhelmed by the force of My Love. Be assured
that I restrain Myself from "crushing" anyone with
My mighty ardor. I know precisely what each of My
children can handle. However, it is possible to increase
your *capax Dei:* your capacity for Me. One of the
best ways is to *delight yourself in Me*—taking pleasure in Me above all else. Ask My Spirit to help you
in this endeavor. Your growing enjoyment of Me will
strengthen you spiritually, empowering you to receive
ever greater portions of My Love.

The LORD your God is with you, he is mighty to save.
He will take great delight in you, he will quiet you
with his love, he will rejoice over you with singing.

ZEPHANIAH 3:17

For God so loved the world that he gave his one
and only Son, that whoever believes in him shall
not perish but have eternal life.

JOHN 3:16

For the LORD takes pleasure in His people; He
will beautify the humble with salvation.

PSALM 149:4 NKJV

Delight yourself in the LORD; and He
will give you the desires of your heart.

PSALM 37:4 NASB

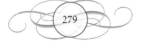

HOPE

I GIVE YOU HOPE—HOPE THAT THE BEST PART OF YOUR LIFE IS NOT BEHIND YOU. Rather, it stretches out before you gloriously: into an eternity of experiences that will get better and better and better. For now, though, you inhabit a world of *death, sorrow, crying, and pain.* Let the hope of heaven empower you to live well in this broken world that is passing away. In heaven *I will wipe away every tear from your eyes*—permanently!

If this world were all there is, it would be tragic beyond description. When *the day of the Lord* comes, I will destroy the entire universe as you know it. And I will replace it with a new universe where My followers will live forever in ceaseless ecstasy. Let this hope give you courage to keep holding your head up high as you endure suffering and sorrow.

The best part of your life lies ahead—stored up for you in heaven, awaiting your arrival. This is true for all Christians, both young and old. As you grow older and deal with infirmities, you may feel as if your life is closing in on you. Physically, your limitations do increase with age and illness. However, your spiritual life can open up ever wider as your soul grows strong in the nourishing Light of My Presence. When you "graduate" to heaven, your soul-Joy will instantly expand—exponentially! *Blessed is the one who will eat at the feast in the kingdom of God.*

And God will wipe away every tear from their eyes; there shall be no more death, nor sorrow, nor crying. There shall be no more pain, for the former things have passed away.

REVELATION 21:4 NKJV

Alas for that day! For the day of the LORD is near; it will come like destruction from the Almighty.

JOEL 1:15

When one of those at the table with him heard this, he said to Jesus, "Blessed is the man who will eat at the feast in the kingdom of God."

LUKE 14:15

RESTING IN HIM

You are My beloved. Although you experience many difficulties in your life, *I shield you all day long.* You cannot imagine what your life would be like if I were not protecting you continually. The adversity I *do* allow you to experience is ultimately for your good and My Glory. You can *rest secure* by trusting that My protective Presence is with you always, no matter what trials you may be enduring.

You must be clear about one thing above all else: You are most assuredly *the one the Lord loves!* In fact, I love you so much that I carry you through your toughest times. Beloved, you can even *rest between My shoulders* like a lamb being tenderly carried by its shepherd.

In addition to being your Shepherd, I am also like an eagle caring for its young while they're learning to fly. Though I *stir up the nest*—getting you out of your comfort zone—I watch over you constantly. When your strength fails as you are "flying" and you start to plummet, I *spread My wings* and catch you on them. I continue to carry you until you're ready to fly again. The better you understand My constant, nurturing watch-care, the more you can *rest secure in Me.*

"Let the beloved of the LORD rest secure in him,
for he shields him all day long, and the one the
LORD loves rests between his shoulders."
DEUTERONOMY 33:12

"I am the good shepherd; and I know My sheep,
and am known by My own . . . and I
lay down My life for the sheep."
JOHN 10:14–15 NKJV

Like an eagle that stirs up its nest, that hovers
over its young, He spread His wings and caught
them, He carried them on His pinions.
DEUTERONOMY 32:11 NASB

INTIMACY WITH HIM

LOOK TO ME AND MY STRENGTH; SEEK MY FACE ALWAYS. While you are seeking Me, I want you to *let your heart rejoice*. This will strengthen our Love-relationship. Imagine an engaged couple who are passionately in love. When the man goes to visit his betrothed, she doesn't open the door and say blandly, "Oh, it's you." Nor does he look past her as if she were invisible and say, "What do you have to eat?" Rather, their hearts rejoice because they are together. *You* are *My* betrothed, and I am the forever-Lover of your soul. When you *seek My Face*, take time to remember who I am—King of the universe—and rejoice in the astonishing Love I have for you. This will bring Power to your prayers as well as Joy to your heart.

I also want you to *glory in My holy Name*. My Name is holy because it represents Me and *I* am holy— perfect in all My ways. My Name is *above every name*, yet you may use it freely to commune with Me and worship Me joyously. You are indeed privileged to have such easy access to Me. Some people glory in their wealth, achievements, beauty, fame; but I invite you to glory in Me—your Savior, Lord, and intimate Friend. Glorifying Me will strengthen and delight you. *Look to*

Me and My strength. Enjoy My loving Presence more and more.

Glory in his holy name; let the hearts of those who seek the LORD rejoice. Look to the LORD and his strength; seek his face always.

1 CHRONICLES 16:10–11

I am jealous for you with a godly jealousy. I promised you to one husband, to Christ . . .

2 CORINTHIANS 11:2

Greater love has no one than this, that he lay down his life for his friends.

JOHN 15:13

Therefore God also has highly exalted Him and given Him the name which is above every name, that at the name of Jesus every knee should bow, of those in heaven, and of those on earth, and of those under the earth.

PHILIPPIANS 2:9–10 NKJV

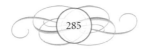

FAITH

I OFFER YOU INEXPRESSIBLE AND GLORIOUS JOY—STRAIGHT FROM HEAVEN ITSELF. This *triumphant, heavenly Joy* can be found only in Me. It is easy for you to slide, ever so gradually, from exulting in Me to living for the next spiritual "high." Though I do grant you some heavenly pleasure while you still live on earth, this is mainly to whet your appetite for the next life. Do not underestimate the brokenness of the world where you live now. Your exuberant enjoyment of My Presence will always intermingle with the sorrows of living in this fallen world—until *I take you into Glory*.

Someday you will see Me face to Face, but for now *you love Me without having seen Me. You believe in Me even though you do not see Me.* This is a most blessed way to live, and it demonstrates your membership in My royal family. Your love for Me—My unseen Person—is not irrational or whimsical. It is a response to My boundless Love for you—dramatically displayed on the cross and verified by My resurrection. You worship a risen, living Savior! *Blessed are those who have not seen Me and yet have believed.*

Without having seen Him, you love Him,
though you do not [even] now see Him, you believe
in Him and exult and thrill with inexpressible and
glorious (triumphant, heavenly) joy.

1 PETER 1:8 AMP

Yet I am always with you; you hold me by my
right hand. You guide me with your counsel,
and afterward you will take me into glory.

PSALM 73:23–24

We love Him because He first loved us.

1 JOHN 4:19 NKJV

Jesus said to him, "Thomas, because you have seen
Me, you have believed. Blessed are those who have
not seen and yet have believed."

JOHN 20:29 NKJV

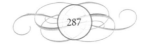

VICTORIOUS LIVING

RECEIVE MY GLORY-STRENGTH. When ongoing problems require you *to stick it out over the long haul*, your faith sometimes falters. That's when you resort to grimly *gritting your teeth*—simply passing time in a negative frame of mind. This is *not* the way I want you to deal with difficulties. I am sovereign over the circumstances of your life, so there are always opportunities to be found in them. Sometimes those opportunities are so obvious you can't miss seeing them. At other times—especially when the journey is hard and seems endless—you have to search for hidden treasure. Do not be like the man who *hid his master's talent in the ground* because he was disgruntled with his circumstances. He gave up and took the easy way out: blaming his hard situation rather than making the most of his opportunity. The truth is, the more difficult your situation, the more treasure there is for you to discover in it.

I gladly give you Glory-strength; it is limitless and freely available to each of My followers. It is exceedingly potent, because the Spirit Himself empowers you—*strengthening you with Power in your inner being.* Moreover, Glory-strength enables you to keep on *enduring the unendurable.* Since this strength has no limits, there is more than enough of it to *spill over into Joy!*

*We pray that you'll have the strength to stick it out over
the long haul—not the grim strength of gritting your
teeth but the glory-strength God gives. It is strength that
endures the unendurable and spills over into joy.*

COLOSSIANS 1:11 MSG

*See, the Sovereign LORD comes with power . . .
and his recompense accompanies him.*

ISAIAH 40:10

*"And I was afraid, and went and hid your talent in the
ground. Look, there you have what is yours."*

MATTHEW 25:25 NKJV

*I pray that out of his glorious riches he may
strengthen you with power through his Spirit in
your inner being, so that Christ may dwell
in your hearts through faith . . .*

EPHESIANS 3:16

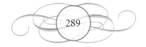

TRANSFORMATION

THERE IS NO VEIL BETWEEN YOUR FACE AND MINE. As you gaze upon My radiant perfection, you *are being transformed into My likeness.* Focusing on Me sounds like an easy assignment, but—as you know— it is not. The world, the flesh (fallen nature), and the devil all conspire to distract you from Me: Godless people seek to delete any reminders of Me from public places, from schools—even from Christmas! Your mind, already in a fallen condition, is relentlessly exposed to unbiblical media messages. At the root of all this opposition is your enemy, the devil. *Resist him, steadfast in the faith.*

I understand your weakness and the fierceness of the battles you face. I rejoice in your desire to contemplate Me and *reflect My Glory.* Having planted that longing in your heart, I want to see it flourish. Take time, take time with Me. Refuse to be discouraged by distractions and the fickleness of your mind. Simply return your focus to Me whenever you realize it has wandered. As you wait persistently in My Presence, ask the Spirit to help you. Little by little, He will *conform you to My likeness.* You may be unaware of these changes, because self-forgetfulness grows through focusing on

Me. Increasingly, though, My Glory will reflect from you—pointing others toward Me.

And we, who with unveiled faces all reflect
the Lord's glory, are being transformed into
his likeness with ever-increasing glory, which
comes from the Lord, who is the Spirit.
2 CORINTHIANS 3:18

Resist him [your adversary the devil], steadfast
in the faith, knowing that the same sufferings are
experienced by your brotherhood in the world.
1 PETER 5:9 NKJV

The LORD is good to those whose hope is in him,
to the one who seeks him; it is good to wait
quietly for the salvation of the LORD.
LAMENTATIONS 3:25–26

For those God foreknew he also predestined
to be conformed to the likeness of his Son, that
he might be the firstborn among many brothers.
ROMANS 8:29

DEPENDING ON HIM

I WANT YOU TO BE ALL MINE. Your security rests in Me alone: not in other people, not in circumstances. However, you are not yet weaned from other dependencies: You want to depend on helpful people and favorable circumstances, as well as Me.

I am not asking you to become a hermit or otherwise isolate yourself from other people. On the contrary, I want My children to help and love one another. One of the main ways I bless people is through the loving acts of others. However, you need to remember that *every good and perfect gift* is ultimately from Me, even if it comes to you through human hands.

The main danger of misplaced dependence is that it can border on idolatry. If you let your basic well-being depend on another person's behavior, you elevate that person to a position that only I should occupy. This is not only displeasing to Me, it is destructive. Because people are imperfect and unpredictable, your life may come to resemble a roller-coaster ride: subject to the whims and moods of another. Even worse, your intimacy with Me will be hindered by your preoccupation with someone else. I deserve first place in your heart!

I want you to *rejoice in Me always*, in all kinds of

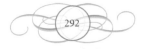

circumstances. You may ask freely for whatever you desire, bringing Me your *petitions with thanksgiving.* Regardless of how I answer your requests, this prayer transaction comes with a promise: *My Peace will guard your heart and your mind*, keeping you close to Me.

Every good and perfect gift is from above, coming down from the Father of the heavenly lights . . .
JAMES 1:17

Yet I hold this against you:
You have forsaken your first love.
REVELATION 2:4

Rejoice in the Lord always. . . . Do not be anxious about anything, but in everything, by prayer and petition, with thanksgiving, present your requests to God. And the peace of God, which transcends all understanding, will guard your hearts and your minds in Christ Jesus.
PHILIPPIANS 4:4–7

LISTENING TO HIM

LISTEN TO ME! Thus you can *live in peace and safety, unafraid*. Listening to Me is the way of wisdom. I make wisdom available to everyone who is willing to hear Me. *Wisdom calls aloud in the street, she raises her voice in the public squares*—proclaiming the truth openly. Those who ignore her message will cry out for mercy on the day of judgment, but it will be too late. *Now* is the time to listen!

It is vital for you to hear Me accurately and consistently. If you hear Me inaccurately, you may find yourself worshiping a false god: practicing idolatry. The best safeguard against this deadly deception is studying My Word and meditating on it. As you do so, Scripture takes root and flourishes within you—changing the way you think. My Word *is living and powerful, sharper than any two-edged sword*—able to accomplish great things in you.

Listening to Me consistently is both a discipline and a matter of the heart. The more convinced you are of My Love for you, the more motivated you are to listen. I have deep, *unfailing Love* for all who know Me as Savior-God. Look up to Me through eyes of faith, and see My Face shining on you with loving approval. *Listen to Me*, for this is the way of Peace.

All who listen to me shall live
in peace and safety, unafraid.
PROVERBS 1:33 TLB

Wisdom calls aloud in the street, she raises her
voice in the public squares; . . . in the gateways of the
city she makes her speech: . . . How long will mockers
delight in mockery and fools hate knowledge?
PROVERBS 1:20–22

For the word of God is living and powerful,
and sharper than any two-edged sword, piercing
even to the division of soul and spirit, and of
joints and marrow, and is a discerner of the
thoughts and intents of the heart.
HEBREWS 4:12 NKJV

Let your face shine on your servant; save
me in your unfailing love.
PSALM 31:16

295

ENDURANCE

I AM FAITHFUL: I WILL NOT LET YOU BE
TEMPTED BEYOND WHAT YOU CAN BEAR. Find
comfort and hope in this powerful promise. I know you
sometimes feel as if you're at the outer limits of your
endurance. Nonetheless, I am present in the midst of
your struggles—available to help you.

Every trial that comes into your life can either
strengthen you (if you keep on trusting in My care)
or become a temptation to sin (if you choose instead
to doubt Me and go your own way). Thus, any diffi-
culty you face becomes a test of your faith. This faith
of yours is *much more precious than gold,* and it grows
deeper through the testing process. So your trials contain meaning and purpose.

When you feel as if your faith is being stretched to
the breaking point, it's helpful to remember that what
you're experiencing is *common to man.* You have not
been uniquely singled out to endure adversity; suffering is inevitable in a fallen world. The most important
thing to remember is that *I am faithful*—totally worthy of your trust in all situations. I know exactly how
much you can bear, and I set limits to your suffering.
Do not multiply your trouble by projecting it into the

future as if it were endless, for I can relieve or remove it at any moment. Your job is to continue trusting Me in the present, waiting for Me to *provide a way out*—in My way and timing! As you wait in My Presence, *be of good courage. I will strengthen your heart.*

No temptation has seized you except what is common to man. And God is faithful; he will not let you be tempted beyond what you can bear. But when you are tempted, he will also provide a way out so that you can stand up under it.
1 CORINTHIANS 10:13

That the genuineness of your faith, being much more precious than gold that perishes, though it is tested by fire, may be found to praise, honor, and glory at the revelation of Jesus Christ.
1 PETER 1:7 NKJV

Wait on the LORD; be of good courage, and He shall strengthen your heart; wait, I say, on the LORD!
PSALM 27:14 NKJV

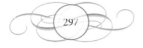

RENEWING YOUR MIND

I REDEEM YOU FROM HELL—CROWNING YOU WITH LOVE AND MERCY; I WRAP YOU IN GOODNESS AND RENEW YOUR YOUTH. I delight in giving you these marvelous gifts because *I take pleasure in you.* Let My delight in you sink into the depths of your being. This satisfies your soul as nothing else can. Although I see your sins and flaws, my perfect Love for you never waivers. I see you first and foremost as My redeemed one—wearing *a paradise crown* and *wrapped in beauty eternal.*

I want your identity as My beloved to be front and center in your mind. However, your thoughts often get stuck on trivial matters, especially when your mind is in neutral. This is why I urge you to *be alert and always keep on praying.* In fact, praying is one of the most effective ways to keep your mind well-focused. As you face your circumstances here and now, invite Me to enter into them. Bring Me whatever you are doing, thinking, feeling; stay in conversation with Me. This will help you focus not on trivial matters but on glorious realities. While you commune with Me, I will *renew your strength.* No matter how old you are in years, *you're always young in My Presence!*

*He redeems you from hell—saves your life! He
crowns you with love and mercy—a paradise crown.
He wraps you in goodness—beauty eternal. He renews
your youth—you're always young in his presence.*

PSALM 103:4–5 MSG

*For the LORD takes pleasure in His people; He will
beautify the humble with salvation.*

PSALM 149:4 NKJV

*And pray in the Spirit on all occasions with all kinds
of prayers and requests. With this in mind, be alert
and always keep on praying for all the saints.*

EPHESIANS 6:18

*But those who wait on the LORD shall
renew their strength; they shall mount up
with wings like eagles, they shall run and not
be weary, they shall walk and not faint.*

ISAIAH 40:31

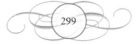

TRUST

A LIFE LIVED CLOSE TO ME WILL NEVER BE DULL OR PREDICTABLE. Expect each day to contain some surprises! I know you greet that prospect with mixed emotions because of your love-hate relationship with surprises. You enjoy the adrenaline rush that accompanies new, unexpected experiences; this wakes you up and takes you beyond your ordinary routine. Yet there is also a part of you that longs for your life to be predictable. In fact, you usually try to arrange things so as to minimize the possibility of being taken by surprise.

I will never limit Myself to doing only what you can anticipate and understand. *My ways and thoughts are too high above yours* for that to be possible. To do so would be to cease being God! So, expect your life to become increasingly surprising as you grow closer to Me. Still, I want to help you become more joyful about your unpredictable journey with Me.

There is actually much merit in expecting surprises. This helps you view an unforeseen event not as something wrong but as something from Me. With this mind-set you are more likely to turn to Me immediately rather than getting upset. You can ask Me to help you find all the good I have infused into the event

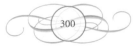

so you can respond appropriately. If you feel unsteady, simply draw nearer to Me.

As you learn to expect surprises each day, your life will become more exciting. You will discover traces of My vibrant Presence in unusual places. Increasingly, you will find your days bright with Joy—the pleasure of knowing Me more intimately.

As the heavens are higher than the earth,
so are my ways higher than your ways and
my thoughts than your thoughts.
ISAIAH 55:9

With your help I can advance against a
troop; with my God I can scale a wall.
PSALM 18:29

And though you have not seen Him,
you love Him, and though you do not see Him now,
but believe in Him, you greatly rejoice with joy
inexpressible and full of glory.
1 PETER 1:8 NASB

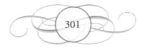

JOY

Be joyful always; pray continually; give thanks in all circumstances. The only way to *be joyful* consistently is to take pleasure in your invincible relationship with Me—the One who rules the universe. This relationship is full of hope, so it is possible to *be joyful in hope* even in the midst of ongoing affliction.

The simplest way to find Joy in Me is to *give thanks in all circumstances*. There is immense Power in praying simply, "Thank You, Jesus." This brief prayer is appropriate for all times and all situations because of My great sacrifice for you. I encourage you to thank Me for every good thing as soon as you become aware of it. This practice adds sparkle to your blessings, increasing your Joy; it also helps you *pray continually*—persistently, perseveringly.

When you are feeling dull or downhearted, it is still a good time to thank Me. This tiny act of gratitude can brighten your perspective immediately. To deepen your thankfulness, ponder specific things about Me that delight you—for instance: My lavish grace, *My unfailing Love*, My continual Presence. Giving thanks in all circumstances is a joyous discipline; it empowers you to *lift up your soul* and live close to Me.

Be joyful always; pray continually;
give thanks in all circumstances, for this
is God's will for you in Christ Jesus.
1 THESSALONIANS 5:16–18

Be joyful in hope, patient in affliction,
faithful in prayer.
ROMANS 12:12

In him we have redemption through his blood, the
forgiveness of sins, in accordance with God's grace that
he lavished on us with all wisdom and understanding.
EPHESIANS 1:7–8

Let the morning bring me word of your unfailing
love, for I have put my trust in you. Show me the
way I should go, for to you I lift up my soul.
PSALM 143:8

ABIDING IN HIM

YOUR STEPS ARE DIRECTED BY ME, EVEN
THOUGH YOUR JOURNEY OFTEN FEELS HAP-
HAZARD. The path that lies before you now is veiled
in uncertainty: You have choices to make but too little
information to see the way you should go. Taking the
next step feels risky—like leaping into the unknown.
The best thing you can do at such times is cling to Me.
Imagine a young girl walking along busy city streets
with a trustworthy adult. She may feel overwhelmed
by all the sensory stimulation, all the possible ways to
get lost. However, if she keeps holding on to the adult's
hand, she will get safely to her destination. Similarly, as
you cling to My hand for help and guidance, you are
ultimately safe.

Though you may not know the way you should
go, you *do* know the One who is *the Way*. Stay near Me,
and you will not go astray. Because I am sovereign over
your life, I actually *direct your steps and make them sure*
even when they feel random to you. Talk with Me about
your uncertainty, your fear of making wrong choices.
Remember that the most important choice you make
moment by moment is to stay in communication with
Me. *This* is how you cling to My hand. This is how you

trust My guiding Presence as you go—step by step—
along the path you cannot see.

*A man's steps are directed by the LORD. How
then can anyone understand his own way?*
PROVERBS 20:24

*Jesus said to him, "I am the way, the truth, and the life.
No one comes to the Father except through Me."*
JOHN 14:6 NKJV

*A man's mind plans his way, but the Lord
directs his steps and makes them sure.*
PROVERBS 16:9 AMP

For we walk by faith, not by sight.
2 CORINTHIANS 5:7 NKJV

ASSURANCE

I LONG FOR YOU TO TRUST ME ENOUGH TO BE FULLY YOURSELF WITH ME. When you are real with Me, I am able to bring out the best in you: the very gifts I planted in your soul.

Granted, being real with Me can be quite painful, because first you have to be real with yourself. When you're feeling bad about yourself, you would rather numb or ignore your feelings than bring them to Me. But *do not be afraid:* I will give you the courage to face yourself honestly.

The best way to face yourself is to remember you are constantly clothed in My *robe of righteousness.* I have no illusions about what lies beneath that pristine *garment of salvation.* Nonetheless, *I take great delight in you*; I even *rejoice over you with singing.*

Open yourself up to *My unfailing Love.* Talk with Me about whatever is bothering you; experience your pain in the Light of My loving Presence. In this brilliant Light you can consider your woeful condition without despair, for the assurance of My Love provides hope. You'll also find that what you most feared to expose is no match for the Power of My radiant Presence. Entrust yourself into My capable care, asking Me to transform you according to My plans for you.

Collaborate with Me as I work on growing the gifts I seeded within your soul.

"Do not be afraid; you will not suffer shame. Do not fear disgrace; you will not be humiliated. You will forget the shame of your youth and remember no more the reproach of your widowhood. For your Maker is your husband—the LORD Almighty is his name . . ."
ISAIAH 54:4–5

I delight greatly in the LORD; my soul rejoices in my God. For he has clothed me with garments of salvation and arrayed me in a robe of righteousness, as a bridegroom adorns his head like a priest, and as a bride adorns herself with her jewels.
ISAIAH 61:10

The LORD your God is with you, he is mighty to save. He will take great delight in you, he will quiet you with his love, he will rejoice over you with singing.
ZEPHANIAH 3:17

But I trust in your unfailing love; my heart rejoices in your salvation. I will sing to the LORD, for he has been good to me.
PSALM 13:5–6

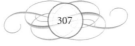

ATTITUDE

I HAVE PREPARED THIS DAY WITH THE MOST TENDER CONCERN AND ATTENTION TO DETAIL. Instead of approaching the day as a blank page you need to fill up, try living it in a responsive mode: being on the lookout for all that I am doing. This will enable you to discover and respond to the opportunities I place before you today.

Many people think they can live independently of Me, but that is an illusion. *I sustain everything by My powerful word!* Not only that, I am your Creator—the Initiator of your very life. Your first cry as an infant was a response to the life I provided. When I cease sustaining someone's life, that person dies. So, living responsively is a matter of aligning yourself with ultimate reality: My sovereignty over every aspect of your life. This can increase your sense of security if you really trust Me. Thus, the art of living well rests upon a foundation of trust—in My absolute goodness, My infinite wisdom, My unfailing Love.

To build on this foundation, you need to be perceptive—seeing things from My perspective as well as yours. Search for what I am doing in the big picture as well as in the details of your day. Conducting your life in this way requires concentration, because the world is rigged to distract you from Me. However, when you *do* succeed in living responsively, you will feel fully alive and richly connected with Me. This is a foretaste of what awaits you in heaven, where you will respond to Me perfectly— throughout eternity!

The Son is the radiance of God's glory
and the exact representation of his being,
sustaining all things by his powerful word.
HEBREWS 1:3

Are not two sparrows sold for a penny?
Yet not one of them will fall to the ground apart
from the will of your Father. And even the very hairs
of your head are all numbered. So don't be afraid;
you are worth more than many sparrows.
MATTHEW 10:29–31

But I trust in your unfailing love;
my heart rejoices in your salvation.
PSALM 13:5

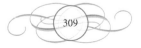

ADVERSITY

I AM NOT A CARELESS GOD. However, when I allow difficulties to come into your life—events that you know I could have prevented—you may feel as if I am being careless with you. In those times, remember that I have fully equipped you to handle whatever comes your way. What you need is: help in using the *equipment*.

My Word and My Spirit are freely available to help you. The Bible imparts to you essential wisdom: My promises to be near you and take care of you, exhortations that help you avoid sinful snares, offers of forgiveness when you "miss the mark," and much more.

It is important not to be surprised or alarmed by the many trials that enter your life. Until you reach your ultimate home in heaven, you will be at war. Adopting a wartime mentality makes it easier to handle difficulties as they arise. You don't waste time and energy bemoaning your circumstances, and you avoid the trap of feeling singled out for hardship.

I do indeed equip you to handle adversity well. But you have to make the effort to use what I provide: My Presence, My Word, My Spirit. *Come to Me when you are heavy laden, and you will find rest for your soul.*

So do not fear, for I am with you; do not be dismayed,
for I am your God. I will strengthen you and help you;
I will uphold you with my righteous right hand.

ISAIAH 41:10

Be self-controlled and alert. Your enemy the devil
prowls around like a roaring lion looking for someone
to devour. Resist him, standing firm in the faith, because
you know that your brothers throughout the world
are undergoing the same kind of sufferings.

1 PETER 5:8–9

Come to Me, all you who labor and are heavy laden,
and I will give you rest. Take My yoke upon you and
learn from Me, for I am gentle and lowly in heart,
and you will find rest for your souls.

MATTHEW 11:28–29 NKJV

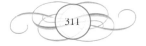

HIS SUFFICIENCY

IN THIS SCATTERED, FRAGMENTED WORLD I AM THE CENTRAL REALITY THAT HOLDS EVERYTHING TOGETHER. When you keep your focus on Me, your life has meaning and beauty. Without Me the world would be utterly desolate—without meaning or hope. I came into the world to show you the way *to the Father*, the way to eternal Life. However, I am infinitely more than a sign pointing you in the right direction. I Myself *am the Way*. Since *I and My Father are one*, I am Almighty God! Yet I condescended to become a man so I could bear your sins and be your Friend. I also wanted to show you the Father's Face—in and through Me.

Everything you need is concentrated in Me. Truth is in short supply in the world, but *I am the Truth*. As you fill your heart and mind with the wonders of My glorious Being, I keep your mind in bright focus—driving back the darkness of worldly thinking. This creates sacred space within you—space where My very Life can thrive.

There is no way to eternal Life besides Me, but you need no other way. Why would you want to follow a manmade path when My *path of Life* is wide open before you? This path glows with My radiant Presence, and it stretches all the way into eternity. As you persevere along this way with Me, I give you samples of *forevermore-pleasures.*

Jesus answered, "I am the way and the truth and the life. No one comes to the Father except through me."
JOHN 14:6

"I and My Father are one."
JOHN 10:30 NKJV

The Son is the radiance of God's glory and the exact representation of his being, sustaining all things by his powerful word . . .
HEBREWS 1:3

You will show me the path of life; in Your presence is fullness of joy; at Your right hand are pleasures forevermore.
PSALM 16:11 NKJV

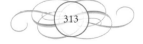

PROTECTION

DO NOT DREAD WALKING THROUGH THE VALLEY OF THE SHADOW OF DEATH. My radiant Presence shines brightly in that *deep, sunless valley*—strengthening, encouraging, and comforting you. Beloved, there is no valley or pit so deep and dark that I cannot see all the way to the bottom of it. Even if you wander from Me and fall into a *slimy pit*, you need not despair. When you cry out to Me, I will lift you *out of the mud and mire* and *set your feet on a rock*—giving you *a firm place to stand*.

Whenever you start to feel afraid, remember that I—your Shepherd—am armed. I am never without My rod of protection, and I use it with deadly accuracy. My shepherd's staff is for guiding you. The hooked end of the staff is perfect for pulling you back from danger or rescuing you when you have fallen out of arm's reach. Find comfort in the constant protection and guidance I provide.

As you face your fears, remember that I am the One who *goes before you and will be with you*; *I will never leave you*. While you are walking through the valley of adversity, let these ten short words cascade through your mind: *I will fear no evil, for You are with me.*

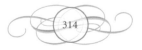

Yes, though I walk through the [deep, sunless] valley
of the shadow of death, I will fear or dread no evil,
for You are with me; Your rod [to protect] and Your
staff [to guide], they comfort me.

PSALM 23:4 AMP

I waited patiently for the LORD; he turned to me
and heard my cry. He lifted me out of the slimy pit,
out of the mud and mire; he set my feet on a rock
and gave me a firm place to stand.

PSALM 40:1–2

"I am the good shepherd. The good
shepherd gives His life for the sheep."

JOHN 10:11 NKJV

The LORD himself goes before you and will be with
you; he will never leave you nor forsake you.
Do not be afraid; do not be discouraged.

DEUTERONOMY 31:8

RENEWING YOUR MIND

WHATEVER IS TRUE, NOBLE, RIGHT, PURE, LOVELY, ADMIRABLE—THINK ABOUT SUCH THINGS. You live in a world where media direct your attention to what is false, degrading, wrong, impure, ugly. Truth has been displaced by "spin," and sensational stories attract advertisers. It is no accident that "true" is the first adjective in this list of excellent qualities. Without truth, there is nothing worth pondering. That is why it's essential to fill your mind with Scripture—developing a biblical worldview.

Even though there is so much brokenness in the world, you can still find much that is *excellent or praiseworthy* in it. Search for such things as for buried treasure. When you unearth something lovely, meditate on it and praise Me for it. Tell others about such things; help them find beauty and meaning in their lives.

True, noble, admirable things can still be found in many places on earth, but they are most abundantly available in Me. So I urge you to *fix your thoughts on Me* as much as you can. Whisper My Name to remind yourself that I am always within "whispering distance." Look at the world around you through eyes of gratitude; thank Me for the many good things you can see. Bring Me your problems as well as your praises, and watch Me transform trouble into something praiseworthy.

Whatever is true, whatever is noble, whatever is right, whatever is pure, whatever is lovely, whatever is admirable—if anything is excellent or praiseworthy— think about such things.
PHILIPPIANS 4:8

Therefore, holy brothers, who share in the heavenly calling, fix your thoughts on Jesus, the apostle and high priest whom we confess.
HEBREWS 3:1

He shall call upon Me, and I will answer him; I will be with him in trouble; I will deliver him and honor him.
PSALM 91:15 NKJV

HIS LOVE

THOUGH THE MOUNTAINS BE SHAKEN AND THE HILLS BE REMOVED, YET MY UNFAILING LOVE FOR YOU WILL NOT BE SHAKEN NOR MY COVENANT OF PEACE BE REMOVED. Nothing on earth seems as enduring or immovable as huge, majestic mountains. When you stand on their heights—breathing in that rarified air—you can almost smell eternity. Yet My Love and Peace are even more enduring than the greatest mountain on earth!

Think deeply about *My unfailing Love*. One of the meanings of "unfailing" is: *inexhaustible*. No matter how needy you are or how many times you fail Me, My supply of Love for you will never run low. Another meaning of "unfailing" is: *constant*. I do not love you more on days when you perform well, nor do I love you less when you fail miserably. My Love is more persistent, invariable, and steadfast than you can comprehend. Open your heart to receive this amazing gift in full measure.

My covenant of Peace is a sovereign gift of grace, and it is utterly secure. I can no more withdraw this blessing from you than I can stop being God. Moreover, *I Myself am your Peace*. So the more intimately you

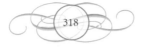

know Me, the more you can experience My unfathomable Peace. Take time, take time to draw near Me; seek Me in the moments of your life. Come freely into My Presence even when you are feeling bad about yourself. Remember who I am—*the Lord who has compassion on you.*

"*Though the mountains be shaken and the hills be removed, yet my unfailing love for you will not be shaken nor my covenant of peace be removed,*" *says the Lord, who has compassion on you.*
Isaiah 54:10

Lift up your eyes to the heavens, look at the earth beneath; the heavens will vanish like smoke, the earth will wear out like a garment and its inhabitants die like flies. But my salvation will last forever, my righteousness will never fail.
Isaiah 51:6

For He Himself is our peace, who has made both one, and has broken down the middle wall of separation.
Ephesians 2:14 NKJV

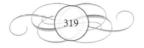

319

SELF-CONTROL

BE ANGRY, AND YET DO NOT SIN; DO NOT LET THE SUN GO DOWN ON YOUR ANGER. Although this is a biblical command, anger is treated as taboo in many Christian circles. Repression of this normal, human emotion is neither righteous nor healthy; in fact, it can lead to serious problems. If you fail to recognize your anger, you are likely to *let the sun go down on it* and take it to bed. This *gives the devil an opportunity*—a place of entrance into your life. It can also result in various health problems. Therefore, early recognition of these powerful feelings is vital. The command *Be angry* gives you permission to have such feelings, so you are free to face them openly. You do, however, need to be careful how you express them.

The first step is to bring your anger to Me. I will help you discern whether or not it is legitimate. If it is, then I will help you figure out what to do about it. Anger can be a signal that something is wrong and needs to be addressed. Sometimes, though, your wrathful feelings are based on distortions: misunderstandings or misinterpretations. Recognizing such distortions can be very freeing. If you have not acted on these feelings in hurtful ways, you can simply release them. However,

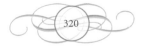

if you have dealt with your anger in sinful ways, you will need to ask forgiveness of Me and anyone else you have hurt.

Remember that I came to *make you free*. Dealing with anger in a responsible way frees you to live abundantly, enjoying My Presence more fully.

Be angry, and yet do not sin; do not let the sun go down on your anger, and do not give the devil an opportunity.
EPHESIANS 4:26–27 NASB

Against you, you only, have I sinned and done what is evil in your sight, so that you are proved right when you speak and justified when you judge.
PSALM 51:4

And you shall know the truth, and the truth shall make you free.
JOHN 8:32 NKJV

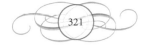

TRUST

I am your Strength and your Shield. I continually work—sometimes in wondrous ways—to help and protect you. As you put your trust in Me, your heart can *leap for Joy!*

Trusting Me and loving Me go hand in hand. When I search the hearts of My children, what I focus on most of all is the measure of love and trust within them. If you say you love Me but you do not really trust Me—to take care of you and your loved ones, providing what is best in your lives—then your words ring hollow.

To trust Me wholeheartedly, you must rest in My sovereignty: My absolute control over the universe. When circumstances seem to be spinning out of control, it's essential to believe I know what I am doing. I orchestrate every event of your life—including suffering and loss—to benefit you in this world and the next. While you are in the throes of adversity, your greatest challenge is to keep trusting that I am both sovereign and good. Do not expect to understand My ways. *For as the heavens are higher than the earth, so are My ways higher than yours.* The best response is simply to thank Me, believing I can bring much good out of the

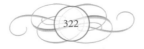

unwanted circumstances. This act of faith will encourage you and glorify Me. I rejoice when My struggling children *give thanks to Me in song.*

The Lord is my strength and my shield; my heart trusts in him, and I am helped. My heart leaps for joy and I will give thanks to him in song.

PSALM 28:7

I love you, O Lord, my strength. The Lord is my rock, my fortress and my deliverer; my God is my rock, in whom I take refuge. He is my shield and the horn of my salvation, my stronghold.

PSALM 18:1–2

For as the heavens are higher than the earth, so are My ways higher than your ways, and My thoughts than your thoughts.

ISAIAH 55:9 NKJV

CONDEMNATION

THERE IS NO CONDEMNATION IN MY PRESENCE, FOR I VIEW YOU ROBED IN MY RIGHTEOUS-NESS. If you focus too much on all the ways you "miss the mark," you can easily fall prey to self-hatred. You need to remind yourself daily that *I have clothed you with garments of salvation*, setting you free from the condemning *law of sin and death*.

I want to help you see yourself the way I always view you: dazzling in royal righteousness. You may find it easier to view yourself this way when you're living up to your standard of performance, but you can never live up to *My* standard—in this life. You need My righteousness just as much on good days as on bad ones.

A common pitfall is to think you can manage your life without Me when things are going well for you. At such times you may feel as if you have no need of My royal robe. Another common mistake is to become so preoccupied with your sinfulness and failures that you despair—forgetting that My salvation-clothing is sufficient to cover *all* your sins.

I want you to enjoy the riches of your salvation, the delightfulness of your guilt-free existence in Me. *I arrayed you in a robe of perfect righteousness* when I

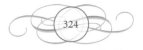

became your Savior. Nothing and no one can strip you of that covering! The more consistently you see yourself clothed in My royal garments, the more you can rejoice in My radiant Presence. You are chosen royalty, belonging to Me—*that you may proclaim My excellencies*. I am the One who *called you out of darkness into My marvelous Light!*

Therefore there is now no condemnation for those who are in Christ Jesus. For the law of the Spirit of life in Christ Jesus has set you free from the law of sin and of death.

ROMANS 8:1–2 NASB

I delight greatly in the LORD; my soul rejoices in my God. For he has clothed me with garments of salvation and arrayed me in a robe of righteousness . . .

ISAIAH 61:10

But you are a chosen race, a royal priesthood, a holy nation, a people for God's own possession, so that you may proclaim the excellencies of Him who has called you out of darkness into His marvelous light.

1 PETER 2:9 NASB

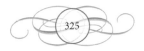

WEAKNESS

BELOVED, THE LIGHT OF MY PRESENCE CAN
FLOW THROUGH YOU TO BLESS OTHERS AS YOU
LIVE IN CLOSE CONTACT WITH ME. So come near
Me just as you are. Through seeking Me and opening
up to Me you will experience My Light shining upon
you—and within you. Let these healing rays soak deep
into your being: blessing you and making you a source
of blessing to other people.

You may wonder how that can happen when you
are so flawed. Actually, the very things that trouble you
most—your weaknesses and wounds—are of greatest
use to Me in helping others, for I have shone into your
heart *the Light of the knowledge of My Glory*. This much
Light and Glory simply cannot be contained within
you! Your wounds and weaknesses provide openings
through which some of this glorious Light spills out of
you into the world.

By letting your humble, hurting parts be exposed,
you allow My Light to shine through you into others'
lives. Thus, your neediness and hurts, consecrated to
Me, become treasures in My kingdom.

*Blessed are those who have learned to acclaim you, who
walk in the light of your presence, O LORD.*

PSALM 89:15

*For God, who said, "Let light shine out of darkness,"
made his light shine in our hearts to give us the light of
the knowledge of the glory of God in the face of Christ.*

2 CORINTHIANS 4:6

*But we have this treasure in jars of clay to show that
this all-surpassing power is from God and not from us.
We are hard pressed on every side, but not crushed;
perplexed, but not in despair; persecuted, but not
abandoned; struck down, but not destroyed.*

2 CORINTHIANS 4:7–9

ABIDING IN HIM

COME TO ME. *Come to Me. Come to Me.* This is My continual invitation to you, proclaimed in holy whispers.

Unfortunately, you're often distracted by the noise of your worries and the clamor of the world. I want to help you *remember* My inviting Presence even when you're too flustered to hear My Love-whispers.

My children so often need help in remembering. They consistently forget Me and the great works I have done on their behalf. For instance, I made a dry path through the Red Sea for the Israelites, saving them from the pursuing Egyptians. Yet many of those former slaves remembered the tasty food they had eaten in Egypt better than they recalled My miraculous deeds to set them free.

Do not let trivial matters distract you from Me. Remember that My sacrificial death and miraculous resurrection shed Light on each moment of your life. I want you to live vibrantly in this Light, increasingly aware of My nearness.

To help in your endeavor to remember, think of Me as the Lover of your soul: the One who delights in you now and forevermore. View yourself first and foremost as My beloved, since this is your ultimate identity. Fill your mind with biblical truth about My perfect Love for you.

Come to Me at all times, My loved one. *Pour out your heart to Me*, for *I am your Refuge*.

*Come to me, all you who are weary
and burdened, and I will give you rest.*
MATTHEW 11:28

*Then Moses stretched out his hand over the sea,
and all that night the LORD drove the sea back with
a strong east wind and turned it into dry land. The
waters were divided, and the Israelites went through
the sea on dry ground, with a wall of water on
their right and on their left.*
EXODUS 14:21–22

*Trust in him at all times, O people; pour
out your hearts to him, for God is our refuge.*
PSALM 62:8

329

DESIRING HIM

I HAVE AWAKENED IN YOUR HEART A STRONG DESIRE TO KNOW ME. This longing originated in Me, though it now burns brightly in you.

Before you knew Me, you tried to find life in many different places. Often you would think you had found what you were searching for—only to be disappointed later. After you became thoroughly disillusioned, I reached down and took you into My own family. Later, you began *thirsting for Me,* longing to know Me at a deeper heart level. You set aside time to meet with Me as your *living God*—vibrantly present with you.

When you set out to know Me more intimately, I rejoiced but I wasn't surprised. I had been pursuing you long before you began your quest. I was working in your life experiences, as well as in your heart, mind, and spirit. Your desire for a closer walk with Me grew out of My painstaking work in you. I initiated your longing for Me, and your response delights Me.

It is important for you to know Me as the Initiator in our relationship. If you think it is your spiritual disciplines that keep you close to Me, you are at risk. Some days you may skimp on your time with Me or not be able to concentrate well. If you're depending on your own efforts to stay near Me, you will feel distant from Me at such times. But if you are relying on Me—what I have done, am doing, will do   you know My Love for you is always assured. So you can rest in Me: *trusting in My unfailing Love*, flourishing in My abiding Presence.

O God, you are my God, earnestly I seek you; my soul thirsts for you, my body longs for you, in a dry and weary land where there is no water.

PSALM 63:1

My soul thirsts for God, for the living God. When can I go and meet with God?

PSALM 42:2

I am the vine, you are the branches; he who abides in Me and I in him, he bears much fruit, for apart from Me you can do nothing.

JOHN 15:5 NASB

But I am like an olive tree flourishing in the house of God; I trust in God's unfailing love for ever and ever.

PSALM 52:8

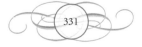

VICTORIOUS LIVING

I WANT YOU TO SAY WITH CONFIDENCE: "THE
LORD IS MY HELPER; I WILL NOT BE AFRAID.
WHAT CAN MAN DO TO ME?" This bold confidence
is not a denial that bad things happen to My people. It
is a declaration of transcendent courage—in the midst
of hardships and dangers. The basis for this courage is
My tenacious Presence with you: *I will never leave you
or forsake you. I Myself go before you and will be with you*
wherever you go.

I am well aware of your fearful tendencies, and I
long to help you break free from them. Most of your
fear stems from pondering bad things that could happen—leaving Me out of that imaginary scenario. This
is a very harmful practice; it is also an exercise in unreality. Although your future stretches all the way into
eternity, there is not even one second when I will be
absent from you.

While the psalmist David was being pursued by
King Saul, he was in constant danger. Yet he was able to
write: *The Lord is the strength of my life; of whom shall I
be afraid?* I am also *your* strength. Whenever your mind
wanders into the future, make the effort to include Me
in that imagery. See Me helping you, strengthening

you, encouraging you. Instead of being intimidated by tough times ahead, view them as adventures that you and I together can handle. If fearful thoughts start closing in on you, push back the darkness with a shout of "Victory!"—confident in the Victorious One who *will never leave you or forsake you.*

So we say with confidence, "The Lord is my helper;
I will not be afraid. What can man do to me?"
HEBREWS 13:6

The LORD himself goes before you and will be with
you; he will never leave you nor forsake you. Do
not be afraid; do not be discouraged.
DEUTERONOMY 31:8

The LORD is my light and my salvation;
whom shall I fear?
The LORD is the strength of my life;
of whom shall I be afraid?
PSALM 27:1 NKJV

ATTITUDE

Do not judge, or you too will be judged. I am aware of your judgmental tendencies, and they grieve Me. Judging is actually *My* prerogative: *The Father has entrusted all judgment to Me.* Moreover, Scripture makes it clear that when you pass judgment on others, *you are condemning yourself.* I realize that much of your judgment-making happens almost automatically—without consciously willing it—and I want to help you deal with this hurtful habit.

Judging others is a classic way of distracting yourself from your own flaws. Ever since the Fall, people have been using this technique to avoid facing themselves honestly. To stop this harmful practice, you need to examine yourself regularly in the Light of My holy Presence. Though this tends to be painful, it can also be a rich blessing. In My brilliant Light you see many ways in which you fall short of My holy standard. This heightened awareness highlights your need of a great Savior and points you to My sacrificial provision. As you ponder the blood-bought miracle of eternal Life— My free gift to believers—you receive My Joy in full measure. Let this overflowing mirth stream through you, washing away *the plank in your eye.* This will enable you to see others clearly—from My perspective.

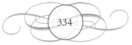

Then you can help them remove their "specks" as you love them with My Love.

"Do not judge, or you too will be judged. For in the same way you judge others, you will be judged, and with the measure you use, it will be measured to you."
LUKE 7:1–2

Moreover, the Father judges no one, but has entrusted all judgment to the Son.
JOHN 5:22

You, therefore, have no excuse, you who pass judgment on someone else, for at whatever point you judge the other, you are condemning yourself, because you who pass judgment do the same things.
ROMANS 2:1

And why do you look at the speck in your brother's eye, but do not perceive the plank in your own eye? Or how can you say to your brother, "Brother, let me remove the speck that is in your eye," when you yourself do not see the plank that is in your own eye? Hypocrite! First remove the plank from your own eye, and then you will see clearly to remove the speck that is in your brother's eye.
LUKE 6:41–42 NKJV

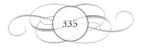

WORSHIP

GREAT IS MY LOVE, REACHING TO THE HEAVENS; MY FAITHFULNESS REACHES TO THE SKIES. You can feel wonderfully secure in Love that has no limits—no boundaries beyond which it ceases to exist. My faithfulness also has no bounds, so it will never run short. Your best response to these marvelous gifts is worship.

I take much pleasure in your praise, which blesses both Me and you—putting you into proper alignment with My glorious Presence. The more you praise Me, the more you will be able to reflect My Glory *among the peoples*. This is the work of the Holy Spirit, who is *transforming you into My likeness with ever-increasing Glory*. As you draw near Me through worship, I change you profoundly—empowering you to make Me known to others.

My Love not only reaches to the heavens but also descends upon you from heavenly realms. Trust Me, beloved, and keep looking up to Me. See Me smiling down on you in radiant approval. My boundless Love falls continuously upon you like heavenly snowflakes—melting into your body and soul. No matter how difficult your circumstances may be, this Love is sufficient to sustain you. Someday you will even ascend to heaven on it! I eagerly await the time when *I will take you into Glory*—to be with Me forever in the perfection of paradise.

*I will praise you, O LORD, among the nations;
I will sing of you among the peoples. For great is
your love, reaching to the heavens; your
faithfulness reaches to the skies.*
PSALM 57:9–10

*And we, who with unveiled faces all reflect
the Lord's glory, are being transformed into his
likeness with ever-increasing glory, which comes
from the Lord, who is the Spirit.*
2 CORINTHIANS 3:18

*Yet I am always with you; you hold me by my
right hand. You guide me with your counsel, and
afterward you will take me into glory.*
PSALM 73:23–24

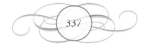

ADVERSITY

WHEN THE JOURNEY YOU ARE ON FEELS
OVERWHELMING, THE VERY BEST THING YOU
CAN DO IS CLING TO ME. At such times the future
seems unreal—unreachable—and the past feels
remote, but this can actually be a blessing. My followers tend to waste vast quantities of time and energy
thinking about past and future matters. Thus they
neglect the present—where they actually live—and
My Presence, though I am always near.

When adverse circumstances surround you and
seem to be closing in on you, it is still possible to *be joyful in Me, your Savior.* Since you cannot find a way out
of your circumstances, accept the situation and search
for Me in the midst of it.

Sometimes you may feel as if you can hold on to
Me no longer. I remind you, though, that you have
been able to *cling to Me to this day.* You have powerful backup because the Holy Spirit lives in you. He can
give you supernatural strength, far beyond your own.
In addition to this, My hand has an eternal grip on
yours. Though your strength to keep holding on may
run out, Mine never will. *So do not fear, for I—your
God—am with you. I will strengthen you and help you; I
will uphold you with My righteous right hand.*

But cling to the Lord your God
as you have done to this day.
JOSHUA 23:8 AMP

Though the fig tree does not bud and there are no
grapes on the vines, though the olive crop fails and
the fields produce no food, though there are no sheep
in the pen and no cattle in the stalls, yet I will rejoice
in the LORD, I will be joyful in God my Savior.
HABAKKUK 3:17–18

My soul clings to you; your right hand upholds me.
PSALM 63:8

So do not fear, for I am with you; do not be dismayed,
for I am your God. I will strengthen you and help you;
I will uphold you with my righteous right hand.
ISAIAH 41:10

PEACE

I AM THE LORD OF PEACE, THE ONLY SOURCE OF GENUINE PEACE. I give you this gift, not as something separate from Myself, but as part of My core essence. As you open your heart and mind to Me, My Peace is present—readily available to you. However, this glorious gift is not something you can grab on the run. You need to take time to focus on Me and enjoy My Presence, putting everything else aside for a while.

You live in the midst of intense spiritual battles, and My Peace is an essential part of the armor I provide for you. To stay on your feet during combat, you need to wear sturdy warfare boots—*the Gospel of Peace*. This good news assures you that I love you and I am *for you:* I am on your side.

Many of My followers forfeit Peace because they view Me as someone who is constantly scrutinizing their lives—peering at them through critical eyes. On the contrary, I gaze at you through eyes of perfect Love. When you are feeling like a failure, talk to yourself and tell yourself the truth: My death on the cross covers *all* your sins. I love you regardless of how well or poorly you perform—simply because you are Mine. Rejoice in this *Gospel-Peace*; it is yours to enjoy *at all times and in every way.*

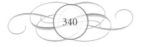

*Now may the Lord of peace himself give you peace at all
times and in every way. The Lord be with all of you.*

2 THESSALONIANS 3:16

*And having shod your feet in preparation
[to face the enemy with the firm-footed stability,
the promptness, and the readiness produced by
the good news] of the Gospel of peace . . .*

EPHESIANS 6:15 AMP

*What then shall we say to these things?
If God is for us, who can be against us?*

ROMANS 8:31 NKJV

THANKFULNESS

SACRIFICE THANK OFFERINGS TO ME. TELL OF MY WORKS WITH SONGS OF JOY! Bearing your circumstances bravely—even thanking Me for them—is one of the highest forms of praise. I have been training you in the discipline of thankfulness for a long time. Yet you still find it difficult to thank Me for suffering—your own or others'. Sometimes you *are* able to do this, and when you do, you find that you relax and feel closer to Me.

Thanking Me for adversity requires a deep level of trust: in My goodness, My mercy, My Love. People who are *leaning on their own understanding* cannot achieve this depth of trust. So, handling difficulties courageously involves relinquishing your demand to understand.

You are learning to endure your circumstances bravely—with thankfulness—and you have experienced personal benefits from this. But there is more—much more! Your grateful acceptance of adversity has major repercussions far beyond yourself: in heaven as well as on earth. Besides having *divine Power to weaken spiritual strongholds of evil*, your sacrifice of thanksgiving rings bells of Joy throughout heavenly realms. On earth,

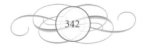

your patient endurance of suffering sends out ripples of good tidings in ever-widening circles to strengthen and encourage My people.

Let [the redeemed of the Lord] sacrifice thank offerings and tell of his works with songs of joy.
PSALM 107:22

Always giving thanks to God the Father for everything, in the name of our Lord Jesus Christ.
EPHESIANS 5:20

Trust in the LORD with all your heart and lean not on your own understanding.
PROVERBS 3:5

For though we live in the world, we do not wage war as the world does. The weapons we fight with are not the weapons of the world. On the contrary, they have divine power to demolish strongholds.
2 CORINTHIANS 10:3–4

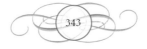

STRIVING

I LOVE YOU REGARDLESS OF HOW WELL YOU ARE PERFORMING. Whenever you're strugglng with performance anxiety, bring those feelings to Me.

Your mind has already unmasked this robber of Peace many times, but the rascal continues to claw at your heart when you let down your guard. You find yourself struggling with feelings of failure, sometimes without even knowing why. I want to help you break free of this bondage through the empowerment of *My unfailing Love.*

Come to Me with your feelings of failure. Bring them into the Light of My Presence, where we can examine them together. These feelings—based on lies and deception—thrive in the darkness, where you are hardly aware of them at all. But they shrivel and shrink in My brilliant, healing Light. All in all, your performance anxiety is no match for me. I defeated this villain in the same way I triumphed over Satan—through My finished work on the cross!

When feelings of failure weigh you down, look up to Me. Let the Light of My Love shine upon you: dispelling the darkness, lifting you closer and closer to Me. The nearer you are to Me, the better you can see My smile of approval. As you bask in this unconditional Love, you gain strength to break free from performance anxiety. Even if you slip into old habits again, you can turn back to Me anytime. My unfailing Love is always available to restore you, because you belong to Me forever.

Turn, O Lord, and deliver me; save me because of your unfailing love.
Psalm 6:4

How priceless is your unfailing love! Both high and low among men find refuge in the shadow of your wings. They feast on the abundance of your house; you give them drink from your river of delights. For with you is the fountain of life; in your light we see light.
Psalm 36:7–9

But thanks be to God! He gives us the victory through our Lord Jesus Christ.
1 Corinthians 15:57

TRIALS

WHEN LIFE GETS REALLY DIFFICULT, DON'T JUMP TO THE CONCLUSION THAT I'M NOT ON THE JOB. *Instead, be glad you are in the thick of what I experienced.* Accept your ordeal as *a spiritual refining process, with Glory just around the corner.*

There are many ways to suffer for Me. The most obvious one is to experience persecution for presenting the gospel to others. However, when you endure any kind of adversity in a Christ-like way because of your love for Me, I view this as suffering for Me. So do not lose heart when the trials you are going through seem endless. You can even rejoice that you are sharing in what I experienced as *a Man of sorrows, familiar with suffering.* Invite Me into your struggles. I understand them better than anyone else, and I want to help you with them.

When your suffering is prolonged, the greatest temptation you face is escapism—trying to get away from your problems at all costs, even irresponsibly. If you endure life's blows in trusting dependence on Me, I can bring much good out of them. I make *all things work together for good to those who love Me.* Consider your trials a part of your education: *a spiritual refining process.* Since you are My follower, your suffering

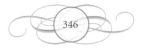

346

will definitely end someday. To help you persevere, keep focusing on the reward—*Glory just around the corner!*

*Friends, when life gets really difficult, don't jump
to the conclusion that God isn't on the job. Instead,
be glad that you are in the thick of what Christ
experienced. This is a spiritual refining process,
with glory just around the corner.*

1 PETER 4:12–13 MSG

*He was despised and rejected by men,
a man of sorrows, and familiar with suffering.
Like one from whom men hide their faces he was
despised, and we esteemed him not.*

ISAIAH 53:3

*And we know that all things work together for
good to those who love God, to those who are
the called according to His purpose.*

ROMANS 8:28 NKJV

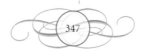

DEPENDING ON HIM

IN MY UNFAILING LOVE I WILL LEAD YOU. Everything else, everyone else may fail you, but I never will. You live in a world of brokenness, where promises and guarantees often come to naught. However, My Love for you is not of this world: It is constant, perfect, and inexhaustible. Nothing can separate you from this perpetual flow of Love, for I have redeemed you—purchased you with My blood. You belong to Me.

The bottom line of your life is that *I am continually with you, holding you by your right hand.* As you follow the pathway to *My holy dwelling place*, be aware that you do so *in My strength.* I strengthen you so that you can persevere in your journey and also glorify Me along the way. Some of My followers bring Me Glory while enjoying vibrant health and multiple successes. Others glorify Me in weakness and ongoing struggles—suffering well in the midst of adversity. Know that I am smiling on you whether your path is arduous or easy at this time. Continue your journey in My strength—which is limitless. I assure you that your ultimate destination is none other than heaven itself!

*In your unfailing love you will lead the people
you have redeemed. In your strength you will
guide them to your holy dwelling.*

EXODUS 15:13

*Look down from heaven, your holy dwelling
place, and bless your people . . .*

DEUTERONOMY 26:15

*Nevertheless I am continually with You; You hold
me by my right hand. You will guide me with Your
counsel, and afterward receive me to glory.*

PSALM 73:23–24 NKJV

*For our citizenship is in heaven, from which we also
eagerly wait for the Savior, the Lord Jesus Christ.*

PHILIPPIANS 3:20 NKJV

TRUST

I AM AN AWESOME GOD! Who but I could be everywhere at every time, ceaselessly working on your behalf? It amazes you that One so great as I would care about the many details of your life. Yet I do! When you ponder these glorious truths, you feel safe, knowing you are never alone. When you don't keep these truths before you, you fall back into your default mode: straining and striving as if outcomes were totally up to you.

What you really need is to keep *Me* always before you—not just truths *about* Me. It's so easy for My children to confuse knowledge of Me with knowing Me experientially. The apostle Paul understood this distinction: He wrote about needing *Power, through My Spirit, to grasp how wide and long and high and deep is My Love—Love that surpasses knowledge!*

Knowing Me is so much more than an activity of the mind. It is largely a matter of trusting Me. Sometimes you are keenly aware of My Presence; at other times, this awareness is minimal—or even absent. When you feel alone, you need to rely on your trust in Me. Continue to live and communicate as if I am with you, because I am! I have promised *I will never leave you or forsake you*. Instead of running after other gods when you feel needy, concentrate on coming nearer to Me. No matter what is happening, trusting Me and drawing close to Me are your best strategies for living well.

I have set the LORD always before me. Because he is at my right hand, I will not be shaken.
PSALM 16:8

I pray that out of his glorious riches he may strengthen you with power through his Spirit in your inner being, so that Christ may dwell in your hearts through faith. And I pray that you, being rooted and established in love, may have power, together with all the saints, to grasp how wide and long and high and deep is the love of Christ, and to know this love that surpasses knowledge—that you may be filled to the measure of all the fullness of God.
EPHESIANS 3:16–19

Keep your lives free from the love of money and be content with what you have, because God has said, "Never will I leave you; never will I forsake you."
HEBREWS 13:5

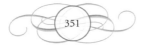

THE FUTURE

FORGET THE FORMER THINGS; DO NOT DWELL ON THE PAST. *See, I am doing a new thing!* I am a God of surprises—infinitely more creative than you can imagine. The universe displays some of My creativity, but there is more—much more. I am making *a new heaven and a new earth.* Moreover, I am preparing My people—all around the world—to live there with Me in endless ecstasy. Let this eternal perspective strengthen and encourage you.

As you journey along your life-path with Me, refuse to let the past define you or your expectations of what lies ahead. You may feel as if the road you are on is tiresome or even a dead end. That is because you're projecting the past into the future. The roadblock you are straining to see up ahead is really just an illusion. The future is in My hands, and I can do surprising things with it!

Your gravest danger is giving up: ceasing to believe I can still do wondrous new things in you and your world. Your assignment is to keep moving forward in trusting dependence on Me. Stop focusing on obstacles you might encounter, and concentrate on staying in touch with Me. As you continue taking steps of trust, expect the path before you to open up in refreshing newness. *I am making a way in the desert and streams in the wasteland.*

Forget the former things; do not dwell on the past.
See, I am doing a new thing! Now it springs up;
do you not perceive it? I am making a way in
the desert and streams in the wasteland.
ISAIAH 43:18–19

Now to him who is able to do immeasurably
more than all we ask or imagine . . .
EPHESIANS 3:20

Then I saw a new heaven and a new earth, for
the first heaven and the first earth had passed
away, and there was no longer any sea.
REVELATION 21:1

Show me Your ways, O LORD; teach me Your paths.
PSALM 25:4 NKJV

INTIMACY WITH HIM

THE MORE INTIMATELY YOU EXPERIENCE ME, THE MORE CONVINCED YOU BECOME OF MY GOODNESS. You've known this intellectually for years, having been taught since childhood that I am good. However, that teaching did not change you significantly. Eventually you became a Christian and tasted My goodness, yet it was only a taste because you still did not know Me very deeply. As a result, when things went badly in your life, you tended to resent My ways with you. Only when you began investing time in seeking My Face did you start to know Me intimately.

You are on a quest to know Me more fully, but I have actually been pursuing you for quite some time. Long before you became a believer, I was working to reveal Myself to you. I placed experiences in your life that exposed your deep need to know Me. I brought you people in whom you could see the Light of My Presence. Even after you trusted Me as Savior I continued to pursue your heart, which was divided between Me and worldly goals. Finally, you began *seeking Me with your whole heart*, and I rejoiced!

Your wholeheartedness has opened the way for genuine intimacy between us. You have tasted My

goodness, and you want more. I have responded to this desire in several ways: I've allowed suffering in your life so that you can learn to trust Me more. Also, I have blessed you with intimate experiences of My Presence—to boost your confidence in My perfection. My goal is for you to become so convinced of My goodness that nothing can shake your trust in Me. Then, *your soul will be deeply satisfied as with the richest of foods.*

Oh, taste and see that the LORD is good;
blessed is the man who trusts in Him!
PSALM 34:8 NKJV

You will seek me and find me when you
seek me with all your heart.
JEREMIAH 29:13

I said to the LORD, "You are my Lord;
apart from you I have no good thing."
PSALM 19:2

My soul will be satisfied as with the richest of foods;
with singing lips my mouth will praise you.
PSALM 63:5

FAITH

THOUGH YOU MAY NOT BE MUCH OF A RISK TAKER, BE WILLING TO GO OUT ON A LIMB WITH ME. If that is where I am leading you, it is the safest place to be. I want you to follow wherever I lead—even if it's out of your comfort zone. I will help you learn to follow me confidently rather than fearfully.

Bring all your fears to Me. Fears that are not dealt with tend to magnify themselves. Expose them to the revealing Light of My Presence, and they will shrink to manageable proportions. Some of them may even appear comical in this Light.

As fearfulness loosens its grip on you, you are freed to follow Me. Grasp My hand tightly as we edge our way out onto the limb. Since I go before you in this adventure, you can keep your eyes on Me as you step out in faith. Soon we will get to a resting place, and then you can look back and see how far you've already come. While gripping My hand to steady yourself, dare to venture a look toward the horizon; enjoy the view from this new perspective!

You are actually safer here—out on this limb with Me—than you would be on the ground. In this new, challenging environment you stay alert: communicat-

ing with Me continually, holding My hand for support. Overly familiar surroundings may feel more secure, but they can lull you into sleepy self-reliance. That is when you tend to forget about Me; it's also when you are most likely to fall. Follow Me confidently wherever I lead, and *the shelter of My Presence will keep you safe.*

If the LORD delights in a man's way, he makes his steps firm; though he stumble, he will not fall, for the LORD upholds him with his hand.
PSALM 37:23–24

Let us fix our eyes on Jesus, the author and perfecter of our faith, who for the joy set before him endured the cross, scorning its shame, and sat down at the right hand of the throne of God.
HEBREWS 12:2

In the shelter of your presence you hide them from the intrigues of men; in your dwelling you keep them safe from accusing tongues.
PSALM 31:20

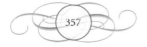

HEAVEN

I AM ABLE TO KEEP YOU FROM STUMBLING. I know how weak you are: how easily you would stumble if I were not holding on to you. I can also *present you faultless before the Presence of My Glory*. You are growing in grace, but complete freedom from sin will not be possible till you leave this fallen world. Nonetheless, because you truly trust Me as Savior I *keep you from stumbling* in the ultimate sense: I won't let you lose your salvation.

I am able to present you faultless—blameless, perfect, unblemished—before the Presence of My Glory because *I have clothed you with garments of salvation and arrayed you in a robe of righteousness*. I want you to wear this royal robe with confidence. You are absolutely secure because it is *My* righteousness that saves you—not yours.

Exceeding Joy is for both you and Me. I delight in you now, but this Joy will be astronomically magnified when you join Me in Glory. The Joy you will experience in heaven is so far beyond anything you have known on earth that it is indescribable. Nothing can rob you of this glorious inheritance, which is *imperishable and will not fade away*. Rejoice!

*Now to Him who is able to keep you from
stumbling, and to present you faultless before the
presence of His glory with exceeding joy, to God our
Savior, who alone is wise, be glory and majesty,
dominion and power, both now and forever. Amen.*

JUDE 24–25 NKJV

*I delight greatly in the LORD; my soul rejoices
in my God. For he has clothed me with garments
of salvation and arrayed me in a robe of righteousness,
as a bridegroom adorns his head like a priest, and as
a bride adorns herself with her jewels.*

ISAIAH 61:10

*Blessed be the God and Father of our
Lord Jesus Christ, who . . . has caused us to be born
again to a living hope through the resurrection of Jesus
Christ from the dead, to obtain an inheritance which is
imperishable and undefiled and will not fade
away, reserved in heaven for you.*

1 PETER 1:3–4 NASB

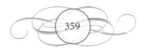

359